PAINTING *and* DECORATING

FURNITURE

with FLORAL DESIGNS

Sarah Sherrington

PAINTING *and* DECORATING FURNITURE *with* FLORAL DESIGNS

THE CROWOOD PRESS

CONTENTS

CHAPTER 1

DESIGN

Design is made up of form, shape, colour and detail. When you look at a piece of furniture, you know instinctively whether you like the design or not. Putting the wrong angles and sizes together is like putting the wrong colours together; it halts the flow of a pleasing design.

Design is ever evolving, combining materials, pigments and paints from the past and bringing them to the present. For artists, crafters and designers, this is an enriching and creative challenge. Throughout history, artists have returned to the rich resource of floral themes and, if you plan to repaint a piece of furniture, then it can be helpful and inspiring to know of the designs that have gone before. A book that I regularly turn to for inspiration and ideas of historically global design is *The Dictionary of Ornament* by Albert Racinet. It is a wonderful book containing an abundance of floral borders and designs. Another favourite book is *Renaissance Ornament from the 15th to 17th Century*, by The Cambridge Library of Ornamental Art. It is a book that is rich in delicate botanical forms and foliage, sometimes depicted in their natural forms but also stylised so the pool of ideas, compositions and colours is immense. Picking out the floral parts of a design from a book or any other resource can help form your own design; you can enlarge it, reduce it, change the colour or link it to a separate design to create your own composition for painting your piece of furniture.

AN HISTORICAL CONTEXT

Baroque design flourished in seventeenth-century Europe and through the ages has continued to attract us with its extravagance and elaborate detail. I have found a wealth of baroque motifs to use for designs and inspiration from a book called *Baroque Ornament and Designs* by Jacques Stella. There are lovely ornate and lavish motifs including florals, leaves, birds, shells, acorns and more, and all are available for reproduction.

The Victorian era was a period of great wealth and power that extended across the globe, and included a rapid advancement in the arts. Designers began to take full advantage of the era of industrialisation, allowing lavish floral designs to be mass-produced onto furniture, wallpaper and textiles.

An early nineteenth-century corner cupboard. The design of the artwork is beautifully 'rounded' to complement the overall design of the cabinet.

A wonderful example of an antique Venetian Baroque-style bed in Italian 1900s lacquered wood. (Image by kind consent of Di Mano in Mano, Italy)

Art Nouveau emerged at the very end of the Victorian era and the beginning of the Edwardian era at the 1900 Exposition Universelle. In Britain, the most well-known designs are by Charles Rennie Mackintosh, where the style of flowing natural forms of flowers, vines and leaves are combined with geometry. Well-known examples of Art Nouveau can be seen at the entrances to the Paris Metro stations. The end of Art Nouveau occurred at the beginning of the First World War.

Artists trying to unite fine arts with a society that was becoming increasingly industrialised created Art Deco, which became the prominent artistic style during the interwar period in Britain and was originally known as 'the style moderne' until scholars renamed it Art Deco in 1968. It represents a design style in furniture, architecture and the arts that, although influenced by Art Nouveau, became a style of its own. Art Deco leant more towards cubism, rich in colour, highly stylised foliage and geometric patterns.

From the Baroque, Victorian, Art Nouveau and Art Deco eras to the present day, fashion has not proved fickle to the longevity of nature in design.

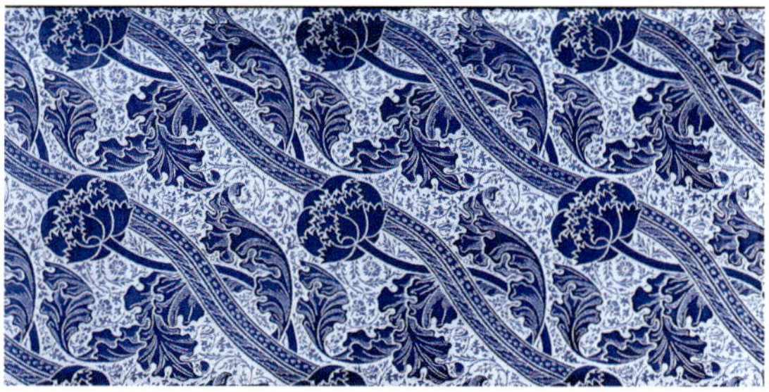

A lovely example of the flowing floral forms typical of Art Nouveau design. (Credit: PublicDomainPictures.net)

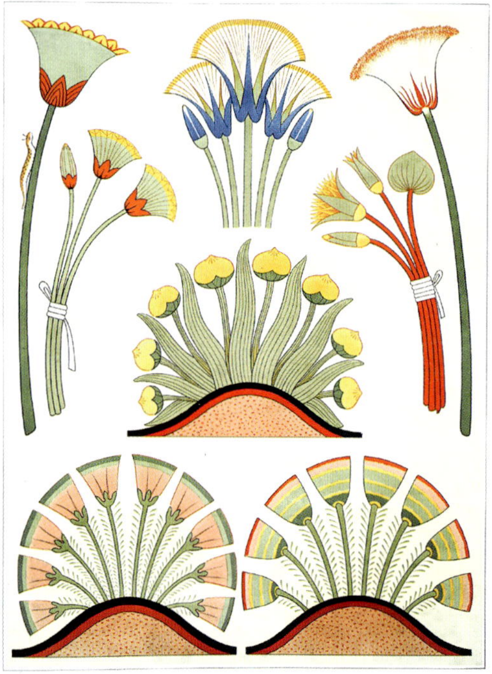

This example of Art Deco design shows the difference in style from Art Nouveau, with its more geometric shapes and Egyptian influence. (Credit: PublicDomainsPictures.net)

It is important to acknowledge William Morris, founder of the Arts and Crafts movement, born in 1834. His love of nature began at a very young age, and he used plants for inspiration in many of his designs. Although he understood, and was inspired by, nature he did not believe in copying plants literally; instead, he used the beauty from nature as patterns for his designs.

William Morris 'Fruit' design. This beautiful vibrant design is still available to purchase from Morris & Co. (Credit: Pictureboxblue.com)

PRINCIPLES OF DESIGN

The word 'design' covers enormous swathes of our everyday life: interior design, kitchen design, product design, flooring design, furniture design, fabric design... and so the list goes on. Almost everything we look at has been designed.

When thinking about how you are going to paint your chosen piece of furniture, it helps to take a careful look at the colours, furniture and designs already in the room. Taking photographs helps, and cuttings from magazines can also help. I have a collection of flowers, leaves and plants that I have left to dry, mainly chosen for their shape, colouring and structure. This means when I am deciding on a design for a piece of furniture, I have a bank of items to choose from. I also keep a large folder of photographs so that if I want to paint something that is out of season, I have reference photographs to use.

Contrast

One basic principle of design is contrast. When someone says that something needs to 'pop' more, it means that more contrast is needed to make it stand out. To put it simply, design is something that looks good and creates an optimal visual experience.

Composition

I look at design as an accumulation of many parts built from observation, balance, shape, size, light and shade, colours, depth and position; all these things go together to form the composition. When putting together a composition to paint onto your furniture, you may find that the rule of three can be helpful. It is the first number we come to where a grouping doesn't have to be formed. For example, if you are painting three pears, you could have two standing and one lying down. Three pears are pleasing to the eye, but you may find that four pears can look cluttered.

Trompe l'œil

The literal meaning of *trompe l'œil* is 'trick the eye' and this technique is used a lot in design to do exactly that. Originally, when buildings were built with very thick walls and narrow windows, there was plenty of wall space inside that could

A lovely example of trompe l'œil, swags of fruit and flowers pinned to a white wall, together with moths and other insects by Martin van Dorne 1770. (Credit: Wikimedia Commons)

Trompe l'oeil effect – using light and shade to trick the eye.

be opened up by painting murals using trompe l'œil. The starting point with trompe l'œil is to manipulate light and shade, and work out which direction you want the light to come from and follow the direction of light throughout. A simple but subtle example of this is to paint a geometric panel using light and shade to trick the eye. I created the following example on the computer, but the design is the same when painted by hand. As you can see, the light on the frame comes from the top left-hand corner, which puts the upper and left-hand side of the moulding in shadow, while the moulding on the opposite side is in the light.

Repetition and Pattern

In design, repetition is one of the elements that unifies a design, such as in wallpapers, in fabrics

Simple pen and ink design of daisy heads in a circle on paper.

Same daisy design repeated on a white background.

With the background of the daisy circles changed to red, the contrast immediately makes the design 'pop'.

A magnolia bud, simply painted with inks and then cut out and glued on paper.

The same magnolia bud repeated and flipped across the page, then turned upside down and repeated again. Both the buds and the leaves form a pattern when joined. A pale green background helped the white magnolia petal stand out.

or hand-painted onto walls and furniture. As an example of repetition, I drew a simple daisy pattern forming a circle, using inks and a dip pen. I repeated the design several times with a white background and then replaced the white background with red, which made the design 'pop'. The white space between the daisies allowed the composition to breathe, while allowing the daisy parts of the design to stand out.

Another example of pattern and repetition started with painting a small magnolia bud. It was then cut out and glued to paper. I then repeated it by joining the bud in pairs and then flipped them upside down to repeat again. The space between the repeated buds creates a sense of rhythm. To allow the white petal of the magnolia to stand out, I replaced the white background with a pale green.

Balance and Movement

All parts of a design carry a visual weight, so your composition should create balance and movement. Movement is the way that your eye travels over the design, so positioning and emphasis contribute to this.

As an example, I painted this refreshing and colourful poppy design using a small sponge dipped in paint. The impression is of petals blowing in the wind, creating lots of movement, and the white space between each flower gives a good balance.

CHILDREN'S DESIGN

The main ingredients for the design of children's furniture are safety, durability and functionality. The furniture should be made from strong and safe materials, with scale, proportion and balance alongside character and perhaps even humour. Pretend play can be created within the decor using designs that engage the child's mind. This example is a short storyboard using humour and characters that small children can engage with.

Babies like strong colours to look at and so this nappy-changing tray, designed to slot

A quick painting using a sponge to show movement and balance. The flowers look like they are blowing in the wind and the white space in between gives balance.

A short storyboard showing how humour can be engaging when thinking about children's designs.

onto the top of a chest of drawers and the corresponding nursery bin, were painted in fun bright-coloured tropical fish for the baby to look at while their nappy was changed. The sides of the changing table are rounded to make sure there are no hard edges, and the fish were painted on the inside and outside of the tray. The whale was painted on the base of the tray so that when it was not in use it was a fun addition to the decoration of the nursery.

A changing tray and wastepaper basket showing functionality and solid design, with the bright colours of the tropical fish used to catch the baby's attention while being changed.

This circular nighttime design is a mural commission painted for a child's bedroom. The sharp outlines add to the strength of the composition and the bats flying out of the circle give it food for the imagination. The white lines of the spider's web balance well with the large bat and the skyline of the rooftops give the feeling of height and space. The blue sky was painted to complement a blue bookshelf that was already in the bedroom.

A mural painted in strong colours for a child's bedroom. The bats flying out of the circle give a great impression of space and the spider on the outside of the circle above the web, with the arched cat on the roof tops, gives added character to the mural.

There's nothing like fairy tales and castles to engage children's minds. I was asked to transform a child's bedroom decor into a castle-inspired theme. The bedroom cupboards either side of this wonderful bed were made from medium density fibreboard (MDF), painted with a faux marble effect, with trompe l'œil arches on each cupboard door.

The child's blanket/toy box overleaf is a fun example of repetition in design, with the repetition of painted soldiers fading into the distance. While being solid, safe and practical, it also offers fun decor and is a strong feature in the nursery.

A commission for a child's bedroom in a castle design showing marbled wardrobes with trompe l'œil arches painted on the doors.

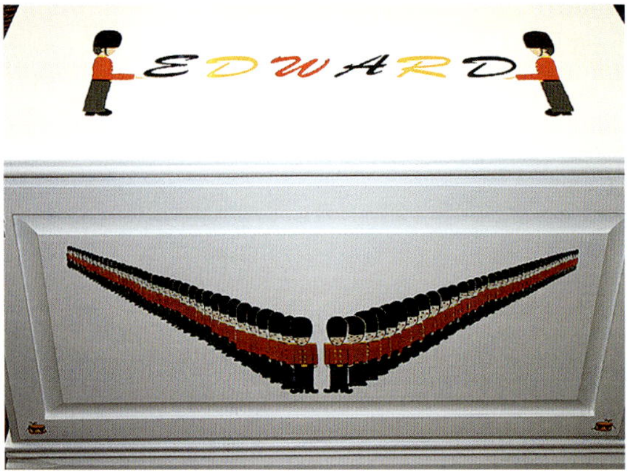

A large blanket/toy box painted in oil-based white eggshell. The lettering was painted in fun bright colours to add contrast to the red and black painted soldiers. The lines of soldiers fading into the distance gave the blanket box depth and form.

Beatrix Potter's timeless illustrations are used to decorate a child's chair and wastepaper basket. The gentle palette is perfect for small children, and allows the furniture to be placed with almost any colour scheme already in the nursery.

The width of the uprights on children's rush-seat chairs is very narrow, so the designs to be painted on them need to be given some thought. Beatrix Potter illustrations are always very popular and, like clowns, they are timeless and classic and the gentle colours of the characters work well with any colour scheme.

These clown wastepaper baskets that were painted for a child's nursery are a good example of movement, character and functionality. Painted in oils, they can easily be wiped clean and the child's name on the front it makes the piece personal to the child. The painted wastepaper baskets can be used on a shelf in a nursery to store cotton wool, nappies or to keep small toys away from younger babies, as well as being used as a wastepaper basket!

Nursery bins with a timeless design to suit both boys and girls. The movement of the clowns juggling balls, both at the front and the inside on the opposite panel, is a great example of combining movement, storytelling and white space, and being personalised also makes them individual. Yet it is such a simple design.

Four examples of using a design on multiple pieces, whether furniture, linen, clocks or clothing.

Once you have your design, it can be used multiple times for different items. You can see examples of the same clown design also being used on lampshades, clocks, dressing gowns and bed linen.

This violet design on a pair of bookends was commissioned for a little girl called Violet. I wanted to fill as much space as possible with colour and movement while leaving enough space above for the name and date of birth. Once I had chosen the design for one bookend, I then flipped it to paint the same design on the other bookend, so that the bunches came from the centre, flowing outwards. In this case, the rule of three works well as a triangle in placing the violets.

Violet bookends showing painted violet bunches coming out from the centre to the outside edge.

Triangle design for violet bookends.

If a design for children's nursery furniture can be educational as well as eye-catching, so much the better. This round, hand-painted table and chairs set was designed as a children's play table, with the alphabet in upper and lower case, plus numbers included. The numbers around the circular edge of the table were painted like a clock to help children remember the formation as they learn to tell the time.

This circular play table and four chairs, decorated with alphabet letters in upper case and lower case and numbers in bright colours, is fun and educational for children.

The berries and fruit design on this mouse clock gives a lovely fresh summer feel to it and the little mouse in the centre gives it character. The numbers were painted in raw sienna, an earth colour, so as not to detract from the illustrations.

The mouse in the centre of the clock would have looked a little lost without a circular border of berries to hold the design together. The stencilled numbers are painted in a paler colour so as not to detract from the illustrated design on the clock.

This Tiger Moth plane design began with a sketch of silhouettes at different angles and is an example of how you can build on and change a design. I added the outlines of poppies and put the aeroplanes flying around and between them as an image for Remembrance Day.

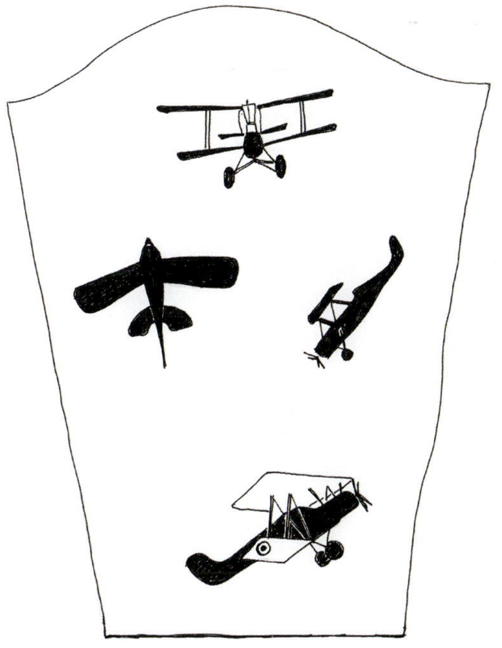

Initial drawing of Tiger Moth planes drawn in black and at different angles to begin the design.

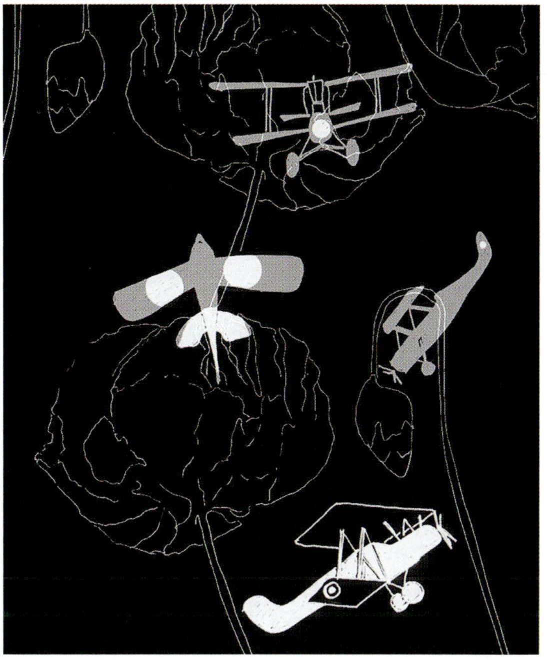

The outline of poppies brought the design together. Then inverting it to make a black background began to make the design more dramatic.

Two Tiger Moths on a green background with the outline of poppies. It looked gentle but did not have the dramatic effect for Remembrance Day that I was looking for.

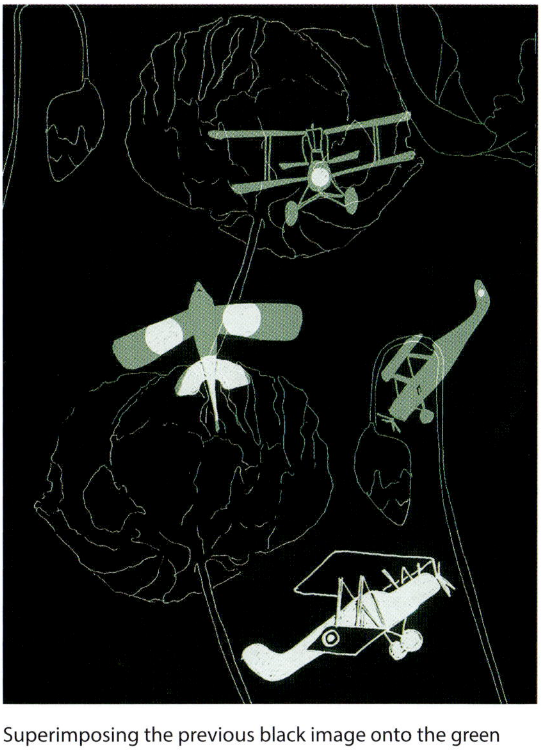

Superimposing the previous black image onto the green background gave a more lively and interesting design.

PROJECTS INCLUDED IN THIS BOOK

The projects that are covered in this book from preparation to completion include the following:

- **Tulip wastepaper basket** with hand-painted artwork (Chapters 1, 2, 4, 6, 7)
- **Coffee table** with faux wood effect and hand-painted artwork (Chapters 1, 2, 4, 6)
- **Chest of drawers** with distressed decorative effect and hand-painted artwork (Chapters 1, 2, 5, 6, 7)
- **Two-drawer chest** with hand-painted artwork and lapis-lazuli-painted knobs (Chapters 1, 2, 4, 5, 6, 7)
- **Children's rush-seat chairs** with hand-painted artwork (Chapters 2, 3, 4, 7)
- **Bedside cabinet** with faux porphyry and hand-painted artwork (Chapters 2, 4, 6, 7)
- **Two-door cabinet** decorated with decoupage (Chapters 2, 4)
- **Stool** painted with furniture paint and stencilled using bronze powders (Chapters 2, 3, 5)
- **Garden coffee table** with Carrara marble effect and hand-painted artwork (Chapters 2, 6, 7)
- **Toy box** with hand-painted artwork (Chapters 3, 4, 7)
- **Small table** decorated with decoupage (Chapter 4)
- **Chair** decorated with decoupage (Chapter 4)
- **Beatrix-Potter-themed furniture** (Chapter 7).

I selected these projects to give you step-by-step guidance in either upcycling or painting a new piece of furniture. The projects are intended to be easy to do at home and give inspiration for your own creations.

Design Considerations

Project – Tulip Wastepaper Basket

I wanted this wastepaper basket to be eye-catching, as it is to go in a spare bedroom and placed beside a mahogany wardrobe. The walls of the room are painted a dusky pink. I chose a dried nigella-African-bride plant for the artwork detail to be hand-painted on the front of the wastepaper basket. It is elegant, tall and delicate, plus subtly dramatic, which was the result I was looking for. Having chosen the botanical piece I was going to paint, I now needed to decide on the background.

My initial thought was that it would look good on a black background; however, the result seemed dull. I then photographed it on a white

Nigella-African-bride seed heads photographed on a black background to help decide on the type of background I would later paint.

Nigella-African-bride seed heads photographed on a white background to check whether the seed heads would stand out enough. I decided it would look wishy-washy although might be good as a design on walls later.

background, just to confirm my thoughts that the creamy white petals would not stand out well enough on the wastepaper basket. It may, however, later be a good design to put on a wall.

I photographed it again on a faux mahogany background, which suited it perfectly. The movement of the reds and dark brown in the background allowed for depth and contrast. This is shown well with a detail photograph of the plant.

Nigella-African-bride seed heads photographed on a faux mahogany background to compare with the white and black backgrounds. I felt this would be the right colouring and effect to choose for the background as it added a two-tone colour effect and more depth to the design.

The overall design for the tulip wastepaper basket is now ready and the next stage is to prepare the MDF bin for painting. *See* the next step in Chapter 2.

Project – Coffee Table

As a design for the centre of the faux wood-grained coffee table, I wanted something that complemented the wood grain both in colour

Choosing a design for the centre panel of the faux wood coffee table. I first tried a fresh sprig of bay leaves. I didn't think the composition or the colouring looked right with this.

I then tried a sprig of dry bay leaves for the central square and decided that the colouring of the leaves and the twig, plus the composition, was exactly the image I was looking for.

and stature. I picked some healthy bay leaf sprays and placed them in the centre to see if the green colouring and shaping would work. However, the green of the leaves didn't tone well with the surrounding colours and any subtlety would have been lost, although I did like the movement and shape. I then tried some dried bay leaves in the centre to see if that worked better.

I preferred the dried spray as the deep reds and browns toned well with the faux wood effect and the stems were 'twiggy', which complemented the table. I also liked the movement of this spray, the fact that there were curls and that the leaves appeared to be reaching outwards towards the edge of the frame, which gave it some movement. I drew a picture of the dried bay leaf spray and traced (Chapter 4) my drawing so that it could be pencilled onto the table ready for painting (Chapter 6).

Project – Chest of Drawers

It was difficult to decide what to do with this rather tatty chest of drawers as it was quite small and had already been spray-painted and stencilled (also with spray paint), and was covered in old stickers. The handles were solid but painted bright yellow with gloss paint, so the chest of drawers needed quite a drastic change.

The first objective was to soften the whole look and so I painted it in a soft chalky white (Chapter 2). On a sample board, I experimented with a water-based scumble glaze, raw sienna pigment and raw umber to make a softly distressed, earthy-looking effect with as much movement as possible (Chapter 6). As the chest of drawers was so battered and worn, I decided that a paint effect would work well to hide many of the defects.

For the artwork to be painted onto the chest of drawers, I chose three poppy seed heads to paint on the top and two further seed heads to paint on the sides. The gentle colouring toned

Cornflower blue chest of drawers with white spray-painted animals in need of upcycling.

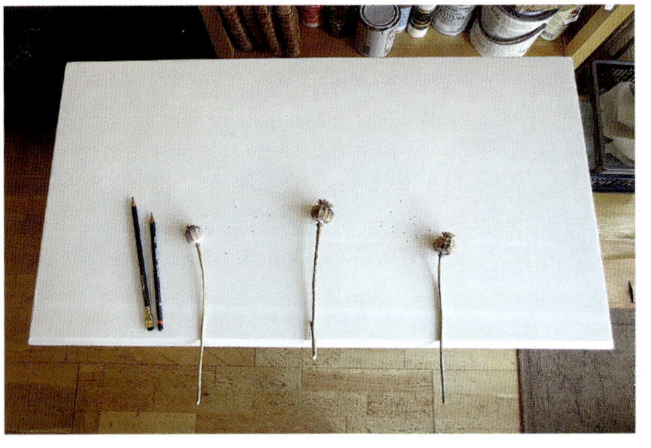

Surface of chest of drawers painted in chalk-white furniture paint and sealed with varnish. Three poppy seed heads placed on top as the idea for the artwork design.

Close-up of poppy seed head with scattered seeds beside.

well with the paint effect, and I liked the idea of the tiny black seeds spilling and blowing onto the surface, adding an extra bit of fun and movement to the design.

Project – Two-Drawer Chest

This two-drawer solid wooden chest with a rounded-edged top and two pillars at the front was crying out to be painted. The handles on the front were either broken or missing and it was looking neglected and forlorn. It was a great size and shape for painting something larger than life and I chose a big peony that was just on the wane. Using a photograph from my photo library I enlarged it and traced it (Chapter 4).

Solid two-drawer wooden chest to be painted.

MULTI PURPOSE
Polyfilla
for all interior repairs
P320
P320

CHAPTER 2

PREPARATION

The term 'upcycling' has only been around since 1994, coined by a German engineer by the name of Reiner Pliz. It is a creative process of transforming unwanted products (in this case furniture) into a new product of greater quality and artistic value. It is the opposite of 'downcycling', which is the process of converting products into new materials, often of lesser quality and value. A big advantage of upcycling is preventing the waste of useful materials by making use of existing ones. This in turn is good for the environment, reducing the manufacture of raw materials, and by doing so, reducing energy usage, air pollution and water pollution.

Although the term 'upcycling' is relatively new, the actual process has been around for centuries and the phrase 'waste not, want not' springs to mind. In folk art, the tradition has long been practised: for example, quilting by the Amish originates from using salvaged fabrics and sewing them together in various shapes and styles.

Painted furniture needs a far higher quality of finish than walls do and is far more intricate to work on. It is sometimes easier to paint the piece you are working on by turning it upside down and working on the underside first, for example in the case of a table or chair.

If you find that the piece of furniture you have chosen to paint has knots, they will need to be treated before you begin to paint. Knots are more common in slower-growing trees such as oak and pine, which is due to the longer time they spend growing large branches before reaching maturity. Knots are a nuisance for furniture painters although they can be beautiful in a natural piece of polished wood. To treat the knots before painting, you can purchase a ready-made shellac stain blocker, or other types of solutions, that stops the seepage through the paint. Sand the wood first to roughen the surface and then paint the solution over the knots with a paintbrush and leave to dry.

Whether the piece of furniture you have chosen to paint is old or new, the principles of preparation are the same. Check for nicks and gaps in the joins, and make sure the item is clean and smooth before you start.

Tools and materials for the preparation of painting furniture. Brushes, Polyfilla, wet and dry sandpaper and a soft cloth.

CHOICE OF PAINTS

You need to remember that if the piece already has a paint colour on it, it will affect the colour you want to paint on top. If you paint a light grey paint on top of a black base, for example, the grey will come out much darker than it says on the tin. If you are painting a paler colour on top of a dark colour, it is best to paint a coat or two of white (or pale grey) first as the base coat. If you prefer an oil-based paint, I suggest using oil-based eggshell. It is very hard-wearing and does not have a glossy shine. You can use artist's oil paints on a water-based base, but it isn't wise to use watercolours on an oil-based base. So, if you decide to use an oil-based eggshell for your base coats, you need to use oil paints for your artwork.

Water-Based Paint

This is a relatively new type of paint with which to paint furniture and has only been available for the last ten to twelve years. Oil paint is gradually being phased out, particularly as the regulations for making paint are becoming stricter and stricter.

There are, luckily, some excellent water-based paints on the market and the quality of the paint is very important to make sure you get a really good finish. It can take a bit of trial, error and experimenting to find the ones that work best for you and the piece you are painting.

Water-based paint technology has created products now that are durable, last a long time and have a very good finish. They are also far better for the environment and, unlike oil paint, they don't discolour (unless bleached in the sun); better still, they don't smell!

The four different finishes for water-based paints are: matt, eggshell, satinwood and gloss. All four of these paints need a coat or two of primer first.

Matt

Matt is a good one to choose if you are matching your furniture colour to the wall colour. It has a very low, if non-existent, sheen. It covers imperfections well, so if you are painting an older piece of furniture, it will hide many of the bumps and scrapes.

Eggshell

Eggshell is a favourite of mine, and I paint most of my children's furniture with it. It is strong, durable and dries quickly. It has a very low sheen and is also a very popular finish to use on painted kitchen units.

Satinwood

Satinwood has a slightly glossier sheen than eggshell. It is a lovely smooth paint and good to use on wood. The 'brilliant white' is a sharper white than the same in eggshell and it is popular to use on bathroom cabinets.

Gloss

Gloss is a much shinier finish than matt, eggshell or satinwood and it is difficult to find a good water-based gloss paint. Oil-based gloss seems to discolour over time and so gloss is losing its popularity as people tend to use a satinwood water-based paint instead. However, if you want a high sheen and don't mind the smell or the long drying time, gloss works very well on furniture.

Gesso

Gesso has been used in furniture painting for centuries, stretching back to the ancient Egyptians, and the recipe that is used today is still much the same. Using gesso fills the grain of the wood and produces a very smooth porous finish, which allows paint to be absorbed without soaking in completely. This makes it particularly good for gilding, lacquer work and marbling.

Before applying gesso, it is best to seal the wood; you can either use polyvinyl alcohol (PVA) or several coats of rabbit-skin glue, both of which are transparent, but I prefer to use an acrylic primer, which is flexible and works its way into the grain well. Rabbit-skin glue may crack over time as it absorbs water from the air, which causes it to swell and retract.

Gesso is a fine white liquid made up of powdered chalk called whiting and rabbit-skin glue. You can either make your own gesso or buy it ready-made, but as it can't be stored it is preferable to make your own. It is best to overestimate the amount you will need, as gesso is built up over several layers. It needs to be applied when it is warm, with the next coat painted on when the previous one has become dull and can be brushed again without being disturbed. However, the coats should not be allowed to dry completely while you are working with the gesso or the fusion between the coats will become weak and prone to cracking.

If small air bubbles appear, tap your bucket of gesso on the table to get the bubbles to rise to the surface and then let it settle for thirty minutes. It is best to apply between five and ten layers to your surface, making sure it is all done in one day, and then leave to dry for three days. Once dry, it can be sanded with fine sandpaper, ideally wet and dry sandpaper used wet, as the dust from sanding with a dry paper is unhealthy to breathe in.

Gesso is quite easy to mix. You will need:

- rabbit-skin glue (granules or powder)
- whiting (powdered chalk)
- a sieve
- a wooden spoon
- a saucepan
- a jar or paint bucket.

The general rule of thumb is to use double the amount of whiting as the amount of rabbit-skin glue; 240ml (8fl oz) of gesso should cover approximately 1.2m (4ft).

Soak the rabbit-skin glue overnight in water. It will swell and form a jelly-like substance so either warm it up on a stove, but do not let it boil; alternatively, add a little hot water from a kettle. Remove any scum on the surface, as if it is not mixed in it will form lumps.

Next, add enough whiting through a sieve until it is the consistency of single cream. Stir the mixture with a wooden spoon to remove any lumps. The gesso is now ready to use.

Chalk Paint

A popular furniture paint now is chalk paint, although it has in fact been around for centuries. The Anglo-Saxons called chalk *Hwiting-Melu*, which translated literally means 'whitening powder'. Chalk's versatility meant that it could be used as a key to white paint, primers or plasters as well as an extender for other pigments. Where there was paint, there was chalk. The Anglo-Saxons quarried chalk along England's south coast, particularly around Dover. There were also chalk quarries found in northern Germany, Denmark and Sweden, plus extensive deposits in Sicily and Crete.

Chalk pigment was found in eleventh- and twelfth-century wall paintings in India. It is such a natural soft rock that the use was inevitably widespread, as well as being easy to quarry and process by using an axe and a sword. Depending on the quality, it was easy to crush and grind the chunks of chalk to produce white powder. It was then sifted to remove impurities and stones, the mineral name of the chalk being *terra creta*, meaning 'sifted earth'.

Chalk paint has regained its popularity due to its versatility and its ability to be painted on many surfaces. It can be easily distressed, and it is excellent for hiding imperfections. It has a creamy matt finish and sands down to a very smooth surface.

There are different makes of chalk paint, which are mixed with different types of chalk; some use calcium carbonate while others use plaster of Paris. The pigments can also vary as some are mixed with natural pigments while others use synthetic pigments. Chalk paint consists of three elements: chalk, pigment and binder. The chalk gives the matt finish, the pigment provides the colour and the binder is the glue that holds it all together.

However, be warned: there are several different brands of chalk paint, and it is best to try them out before painting a large piece. I hate 'gloop' and to my horror tried one recently that was gloopy and stiff and very difficult to use, whereas the same type of paint but a different brand painted on very smoothly and easily and gave an excellent finish.

Oil Paint

It is thought that oil paint was used as early as the seventh century AD, as examples have been found of Buddhist paintings in Afghanistan where walnut and poppy oils were used. By the twelfth century, oil paints were being used for decoration in Europe, as it was good for covering interior wood and metal due to it being so hard-wearing. It did not become an artistic medium until the early fifteenth century.

Oil paint is a slow-drying paint, consisting of particles of pigment mixed with oil, the most common of which is linseed oil pressed from the seed of the flax plant. Safflower and poppy seed oils are also used and are paler in colour, which produces a more vibrant and brighter finish. Oil paint dries far more slowly than water-based paint as when it is exposed to the air it does not evaporate in the same way, instead drying to a semi-solid film. When white spirit or turpentine is added, it affects the flow of the paint, which adjusts the drying time and the consistency. The slow drying time of oil paint is an advantage for painting artwork on furniture. It means the work can be created at a slower pace, with corrections and changes easily made with the use of white spirit. Chemical additives are also added to the oil, which varies the tone of a gloss finish, or helps the paint to dry more quickly. When choosing an oil paint to paint your piece of furniture, do read the instructions on the tin as the makes, sheens and drying times vary. Always stir or shake well before opening the tin.

SANDING

The preparation of the piece of furniture you are going to paint is important and requires a bit of effort to achieve. When you look at a piece of marble, it is not only the visual effect but also the smoothness of touch that attracts you, and this is the same combination and effect to aim for when painting furniture. The size of grit makes a big difference when sanding. I am a big fan of wet and dry sandpaper, which, as the name implies, can be used either wet or dry. It is graded by numbers, the highest number being the smoothest and the lowest number being the roughest. By using the correct grades of sandpaper, you can achieve a very high standard of finish, and there are three basic stages to this. The first is to use the coarsest grade to create a new surface; the second is to use a medium grade to smooth the new surface; the third is to use the finest grade to ready the surface to paint.

It is best to sand in the direction of the grain, and to use the wet and dry sandpaper dry when sanding directly onto the wood. However, wetting it with water keeps it sharp and avoids clogging, plus it lasts longer, so when sanding on an already painted piece of furniture you can use it wet, rinsing the surface regularly to remove any sludge. Always make sure to wipe clean and leave the area to dry once sanded to avoid any sludge or dust particles getting in your next layer of paint.

PREPARATION FOR THE PROJECTS IN THIS BOOK

Project – Tulip Wastepaper Basket

The tulip wastepaper basket is made from MDF. This is a great surface for painting as it is very smooth and as it is man-made it has no grain. It is a wood-based material made from mixing together softwood and hardwood fibres with a synthetic resin adhesive. It is available in sheets of various sizes and depths and, while it is perfect for a painter, it is not as strong as solid wood.

First, I use a damp soft cloth to wipe and clean the item I'm about to paint, making sure there are no hidden marks and to remove any dust. I then check that the joins are good. In this case there is a slight gap between the panels that needs to be filled with Polyfilla before going any further.

I always check the corner joints on the top of the bin as they need to be flush. Using a small lump of ready-mixed Polyfilla on the end of my finger, I carefully fill the joins and the corners, making the end result as smooth as possible. Big lumps of filler don't dry well and will break off, so a second layer of filler once the first one is dry is the best way to do it.

The same preparation is used for the bookends, also made from MDF with the upright panel being much thicker than the depth of the panels on the bins. There are narrow gaps that must be filled, as otherwise you will be left with a black line once painted. Once the filler is dry it needs sanding down to a smooth finish. I use wet and dry sandpaper no. 340 for the first sanding.

Once the filler has dried and is sanded to a smooth finish, the furniture is ready for the first coat of primer. I use a water-based acrylic primer that paints on easily, leaving a smooth finish when dry and sanded. If I am painting several bins at the same time, I often use a small roller for the base coats. It avoids brush marks and speeds the process up.

When the first coat of primer is dry, I sand again, using the same no. 340 wet and dry sandpaper. You can wet the sandpaper first, but make sure to wipe clean soon afterwards so that no residue sticks. I usually use the sandpaper dry and then clean the dust off with a damp soft cotton cloth. Once sanded, the area should be smooth to the touch with no bits of fluff or dust left behind. Then repeat the process with a second coat of primer.

For the final two coats you can either use an oil-based eggshell or a water-based eggshell. As with the first two coats of primer, once you have painted the next coat with eggshell, sand again and then wipe clean. For the sanding in between

MDF tulip bin before any preparation is started.

Detail showing gap between two panels to be filled.

the final two coats, I use a wet and dry sandpaper no. 400 and for the final coat no. 600. You will end up with a smooth glass-like finish that is perfect for painting your artwork on. Preparation is very important for the final look of the piece to give it a professional quality. Poor or uneven preparation with brush marks and dust doesn't look good and won't show off your artwork well.

The gap between the two panels and the top corner are filled with Polyfilla, then sanded with wet and dry sandpaper until the surface is smooth.

The bookends are now ready for their first coat of primer.

Detail of corners and uprights filled on bookends with Polyfilla and sanded smooth.

The tulip bin corner and side filled and painted with one coat of primer.

The tulip bin has been primed, sanded and cleaned, ready for two coats of eggshell.

Project – Children's Rush-Seat Chairs

The carcass of the children's rush-seat chairs is made of ash. Ash is a light-coloured hardwood and ideal for making furniture. It is strong, dense and durable, with good flexibility and therefore very popular for woodworking.

The rush-seat pad of the chair should be removed before any painting is started. It is secured to the frame with brass screws and is easy to take off.

After wiping the chair frame with a damp cloth to remove any dust or dirt, I painted the first coat of water-based acrylic primer using a decorator's brush, size 25mm. Always try to use the right brush size for the area you are painting, as a wider brush on a narrow upright will hold too much paint and make it difficult to avoid drips and mess. I then sanded the primer when it is dry with wet and dry sandpaper no. 340.

Sometimes it is easier to spot cracks that need filling once the wood has been painted with the first coat of white primer and sanded down.

When all the cracks are filled with Polyfilla and dry, sand smooth before painting the second coat of primer. When the second coat of primer is dry, sand again and wipe clean, then paint the first coat of eggshell. Repeat the process for the second coat of eggshell.

A child's chair, made in Italy from hard-wearing ash with a rush seat, before painting.

The frame of child's rush-seat chair once the rush-seat pad has been removed.

Showing the gap on the side of the chair that needs to be filled.

Carcass of child's rush-seat chair painted with two coats of primer.

Project – Coffee Table

The origination of the word table is from the old French word *tablel*, which means *tableau* (as in painted scene). However, tables are rarely painted as such and more often than not are varnished, stained or glossed; yet with a lovely big flat tabletop as a canvas, it is an ideal piece of furniture with which to create an exciting decorative accessory.

The same preparation as for the bin, bookends and chair was used to prepare this coffee table before any decorative techniques or artwork were started. Made from MDF, there was quite a lot of filling to be done after one coat of primer had been painted, especially where the tabletop met the legs and the frame. With a larger piece of furniture, an electric sander is useful for saving time and sanding over a large area, but for small pieces I prefer to do it by hand.

I decided to paint a faux wood effect on the table, with a central square framing a botanical painting that would be painted in artist's oil paint. Once the two coats of primer were done, all the joins and gaps were filled, and it was sanded and smooth, I painted two coats of orange oil-based eggshell as the base colour for the decorative paint effects to follow. I measured out a square in the centre to leave blank for the artwork and other decorative effects, using masking tape to ensure a clean edge was left when removed. *See* Chapter 6 for decorative paint techniques for the next steps.

Showing where the gaps need to be filled with Polyfilla on the underside of MDF coffee table. You can mix your own Polyfilla by adding water and mixing with Polyfilla powder, but to save time I often use it premixed.

The orange oil-based eggshell paint to use for the coloured base coats on the coffee table.

Measuring and using masking tape to form the square in the centre of the coffee table where the artwork will be painted.

The top of the coffee table after being painted with two coats of orange oil-based eggshell before removing the masking tape.

Masking tape removed once the tabletop has been painted orange, leaving a white square for the artwork with a surrounding frame to be painted with decorative paint effects (*see* Chapter 6).

Project – Bedside Cabinet

This pretty bedside cabinet had been painted in a pale grey furniture paint. I decided to paint a large blackberry design on the top to liven it up a little, as there was a perfect frame already around the edge. I wanted the frame to simulate a red stone like porphyry. You can see how the porphyry decorative effect was painted in Chapter 6; however, the preparation for this needed a base coat of pink. Masking tape was attached to the inside and outside edges, to make sure the there was no smudging from the pink on the pale grey when painting. As I mixed the colour using alizarin crimson and white eggshell, I tried the pink out on a sample board first to make sure that I achieved the right tone of pink.

I then painted two coats of white eggshell as a base coat on the top, inside the frame, as a background for the blackberry artwork to be painted later. *See* the next steps in Chapters 4, 6 and 7.

The grey-painted bedside cabinet before further painting begins.

Masking tape is added around the top of the bedside cabinet to prevent smudging when the pink surround is added.

A sample board showing the area painted pink as the trial base coat for porphyry.

Project – Two-Door Cabinet

To make this reproduction games cupboard look a little more interesting and fun, on each door I decided to decoupage a large image of a leaf that I had painted previously as a watercolour (*see* Chapter 4). The doors already had a frame on each side and so there was a perfect space for decoration.

There was minimal preparation needed. As my original watercolour painting had a black charcoal background, I decided that a chalky graphite background for the decoupage image would work. After thoroughly cleaning the square on each cupboard door, I painted two coats of graphite furniture paint, leaving the rest of the cupboard alone. With this paint there was no need for a primer, and it could be painted straight onto the wood

The reproduction cabinet before painting and decoupage.

The panel on each door of the cabinet was painted with two coats of graphite furniture paint in preparation for decoupage.

Project – Stool

This is an old stool where the top was replaced with a flat screwed-on piece of wood, of neither good quality nor attraction. The first step was to clean it all over with a damp cloth and then to fill the screw holes on the top with Polyfilla to make sure they were flush with the surface. I didn't sand the whole top, as I wanted the rough grain to show through the paint I was going to use. I only sanded the areas that were filled with Polyfilla.

The top was painted with a coat of acrylic primer before adding two coats of grey furniture paint, while the rest of the stool was painted in grey furniture paint with no primer. This is because the furniture paint used was water-based and the wood doesn't necessarily need to be primed.

I then wiped the stool with a damp cloth to give it a slightly distressed look, with the golden colour of the wood showing through some of the grey. The top was left dark grey.

The top of the stool was then stencilled (Chapter 3) and metal powders used for the decoration (Chapter 5).

The stool to be cleaned before painting.

The screw heads to be filled and the rough-grained wood on the top of the stool.

The holes and screw heads filled with Polyfilla and sanded down to make sure that they are flush with the surrounding wood, ready for primer.

The stool with a white coat of primer on the top and the grey graphite furniture paint on the rest of the stool.

The white primer on the top has been painted with grey furniture paint. Gently wiping over areas with a damp cloth leaves a distressed look on the rest of the stool.

Project – Chest of Drawers

This small chest of drawers was originally painted in cornflower blue gloss paint, with white spray-paint stencilled animals on top. It also had stickers on, which had been stuck there for a very long time.

First, I washed it all over with warm water and fairy liquid. Fairy liquid is brilliant for removing any grease or sticky patches. The stickers proved a bit of a problem, and some of them took the paint off when removed. The patches of paint that had come off when cleaning left holes that had to be filled before doing any further painting.

I sanded it all over with wet and dry sandpaper no. 340. Using a chalk-white water-based paint, I painted two coats straight on top of the blue gloss. It was difficult to spread the paint as it was thick and gloopy and, although it was the matt chalky finish that I wanted, I had to sand between each coat as the brush strokes were very visible. Once dry and sanded, it was in fact a lovely finish and smooth to the touch. However, because I had decided I would paint a decorative finish on top of the white, I gave it one coat of water-based varnish to seal any absorption and left it to dry.

I noticed that the sides of the drawers had never been painted, which is an ugly look for a painted piece of furniture. Using the same chalk water-based furniture paint, I painted the sides of the drawers and the top edges. If you paint the sides of the drawers and find that they swell a little and then have a problem fitting them back into their slots, the best way to help them slide is by rubbing a candle along the sides, as the wax will work as a lubricant.

For further insight into painting and decorating this chest of drawers, *see* Chapters 1, 5, 6 and 7.

This small chest of drawers was really beaten up and in need of some tender loving care!

A hole left by sanding and cleaning, which is then filled with Polyfilla.

Once the chest of drawers had been cleaned and sanded, and all holes filled, it was painted with chalk-white furniture paint followed by a coat of water-based varnish to seal it.

The drawer sides had never been painted, which did not look good when the drawers were opened.

I painted the drawer sides and top edges with the same chalk-white furniture paint.

Project – Two-Drawer Chest

I found this two-drawer chest in an auction and thought it would be perfect for painting. It is very heavy and solid, with curved columns either side of the two long drawers. The grain is quite open, but it has never been varnished. I began by cleaning it and then painting two coats of water-based primer, using a small roller to avoid brush strokes. The acrylic in the primer helps to fill the grain without needing too much Polyfilla. There were, however, some areas that needed filling, especially on the joins and the sides.

I thought that painted wooden knobs on the drawers would work well and so I filled the holes left from the previous handles, just leaving one hole for each knob on each drawer. Like the chest, I painted the knobs with primer. I then added a coat of water-based eggshell tinted with ultramarine on them, as this is a good base-coat colour to paint a lapis lazuli effect for the finish.

Once I had painted the chest with two coats of primer, and all the gaps had been filled, I used a slightly tinted water-based eggshell paint for the final two coats. The artwork would be a large fading peony, and I decided that a bright white base would look too stark, whereas a tinted base would give a better feeling of warmth and would help the very pale colouring of the peony to stand out.

The chest was now ready for the artwork. Please *see* Chapters 4, 5, 6 and 7 for the next stages.

The two-drawer chest before painting.

There were gaps along the top of the chest and the sides that needed filling.

The top edge where the top meets the base, filled and sanded, ready for the next coat of paint.

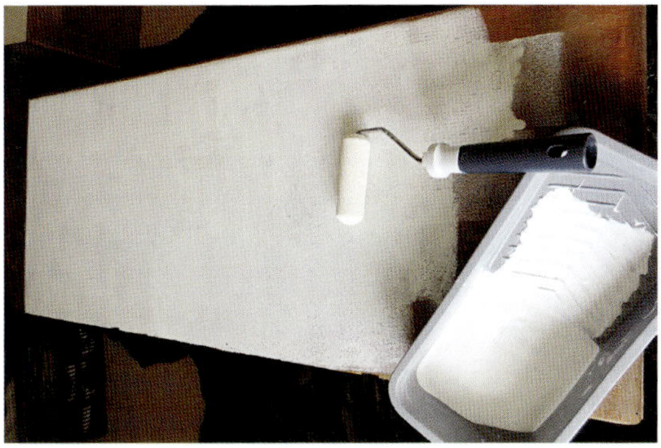

I used a small roller to paint the primer onto the chest; it was quicker and avoided brush strokes.

The chest once painted with two coats of primer and all the joins and gaps filled.

The chest, having been painted with two coats of tinted water-based eggshell, was now ready for the artwork.

I added a tinted base for the peony artwork on top of the chest. You can also see the wooden knobs painted with two coats of primer and then a coat of water-based eggshell tinted with ultramarine blue artist's oil paint as a base for lapis lazuli.

Project – Garden Coffee Table

After cleaning the table with a damp cloth and filling small areas where necessary, I then sanded it all over with wet and dry sandpaper. I then painted two coats of acrylic primer, sanding between each coat and leaving a smooth surface for the spray paint. I decided to use a Rust-Oleum Universal gloss spray paint in racing green for the table, leaving a circle in the centre of the tabletop white to paint a faux Carrara marble.

Spray paint is very toxic and if you are using it at home, either try to put the furniture in the fresh air or make sure that all the windows are open in the room you are working in. I would also suggest that you wear a mask while you are spraying. I put this table in the garden in an area where I didn't mind if the grass turned racing green. Insects and flies can be a problem, but if you spray quickly, and immediately take it indoors after each coat, it makes it easier. If you do get a small fly, pick it off quickly and the paint should spread over the tiny mark it may have made.

To make sure the circle in the centre didn't get sprayed, I covered a plate with cling film, making sure there weren't any tiny holes that the spray could invade, and placed it in the centre of the table. It worked well, and any slight green that floated underneath could easily be painted over once dry with water-based eggshell paint. Once the green was completely dry, I painted the inside of the circle with white eggshell paint, using a small fitch to keep the line around the edge sharp. The table was now ready for the faux Carrara marble effect in the centre and floral paintings around the edge.

See Chapter 6 for the Carrara marble effect and Chapter 7 for the floral artwork.

Placing a plate in the centre of the table after covering it with cling film before spraying.

I sprayed the table with racing green enamel spray paint, spraying thin layers and leaving it to dry between coats until the table reached a uniform green colour.

Using a fitch brush and a steady hand, I painted water-based white eggshell around the circle edge before painting the centre with a larger brush.

CHAPTER 3

STENCILLING AND LETTERING

STENCILLING

Stencilling is a simple and versatile method for repeating a design on walls, furniture, fabrics and windows by using a cut-out shape.

Originally, stencilling used perishable materials and so it is difficult to know when, where and how the art of stencilling first began. There is evidence to suggest that stencilling was used by prehistoric humans from 30,000BCE in cave paintings and it is known that stencils were made from dried sealskin by the early Inuit. Stencils were also used in Egypt around 2500BCE to decorate mummy cases. The Chinese were the first to produce more durable stencils by using paper.

When trade routes between Japan and China opened, the art of stencilling began to spread to other East Asian and Middle Eastern countries, with differing techniques beginning to emerge and evolve. Stencilling in Japan, where the art dates back to AD600, is still a very popular craft, particularly on fabrics, where cotton kimonos are decorated with stencilled butterflies, flowers and birds.

Early stencilling in England was an underrated practice and it is difficult to date, as visual proof is rare. The earliest signs were found in churches and halls in the thirteenth and fourteenth centuries, although they have almost disappeared with the passage of time. There is stronger evidence of stencils being used in the fifteenth century, again mostly in churches on wood, walls and panels and as backgrounds to prominent religious figures.

However, the popularity of stencilling being used in churches came to a halt for almost a century when the Painters' and Stationers' Company of London announced that the art is 'a false and deceitful work and destructive to the art of painting, being a great hinderance of ingenuity and a cherisher of idleness and laziness in all beginners of the said art'. It is thought that this was said to protect the master craftsmen of the day and this powerful announcement from a powerful establishment succeeded.

Thanks to the Arts and Crafts movement in Victorian England, stencilling began to reappear again mostly due to the influence of William Morris and the architect William Burges. Charles Rennie Mackintosh, who with his partners became known as the Glasgow Four, were the driving force of stencilling in the Art Nouveau movement, although their stencilling work was considered unconventional at the time. They exhibited at the Arts and

This commissioned child's round table is painted with the alphabet in upper and lower case, and with numbers around the edge representing a clock face. The four rush-seat chairs also had numbers and letters of the alphabet hand-painted onto the front and backs. An educational, practical and attractive design for children.

Craft Exhibition in 1896 but their work was not well received.

In America, the first settlers that arrived on the east coast became prolific stencillers. Using local pigments, bands of craftsmen would travel from one settlement to another decorating and embellishing walls, floors and furniture with their own designs, thus transforming modest habitats with charm and originality. As settlements grew and became more prosperous, the increase of demand grew with it and so mass production of machine-produced wallpapers and fabrics obscured the delicate stencilling of the previous generation. Between the First World War and the Second World War, the Modernist movement brought with it clean white walls and minimalist interiors, and stencilling was again stopped in its tracks.

Like a roundabout, all trends come and go, and we seem to be emerging from a minimalist era in England at the time of writing. It is gradual, but I sense that bit by bit the arts and crafts are returning after a long gap of around thirty years.

One of the advantages of change is that now we can use water-based paints and glazes, that are safer, less toxic and quicker to use on many different surfaces.

Project – Stool

In the sixteenth century, Spanish Christian missionaries discovered the passion flower and symbolised it as being the story of Jesus. They thought that the three stigmas represented the three nails that held Jesus to the cross, the five anthers represented the five wounds of Jesus (hands, feet and the stabbing to his side) and the filaments represented the crown of thorns, while the vine represented God's attachment to the earth. That aside, it seemed a good geometric design to use to make a stencil and I began by photographing the flower from above to use for reference.

Photograph of a passion flower taken from above to use as the design for the centre stencil.

I traced the outline of a passion flower onto a plain sheet of paper and then filled the areas that would be cut out to make the stencil. Bridges needed to be left between the filled areas so that each cut-out section was separate from the rest.

I wanted to try out the design before I painted it onto the stool, so I decided to paint a sample board. Using a piece of plyboard, I painted a large white square of acrylic primer, sanded it when dry with very fine sandpaper and then painted two coats of furniture paint (graphite) on top. I was going to stencil the passion flower using bronze powders so I decided not to sand the graphite furniture paint before stencilling so that subtle brush strokes would remain and add texture to the images.

Making one larger stencil of the flower in the centre, I then made two further stencils to go in

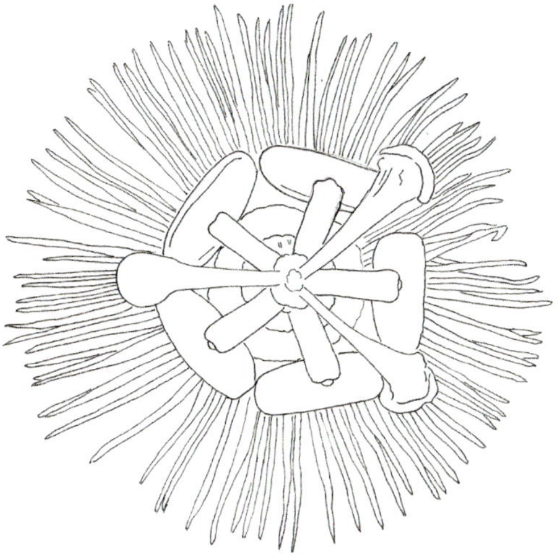

This is the whole design drawing for the passion flower for the centre of the stool, so that I can work out where the bridges should be to hold it together as a stencil.

This black and white drawing shows where the bridges are for the stencil, with the black areas filled in to show which parts to cut out.

Sample board showing a square painted with graphite furniture paint.

Photograph showing the bud used as reference for the design for the first bud stencil.

Photograph showing the second bud used as reference for the design for the next stencil.

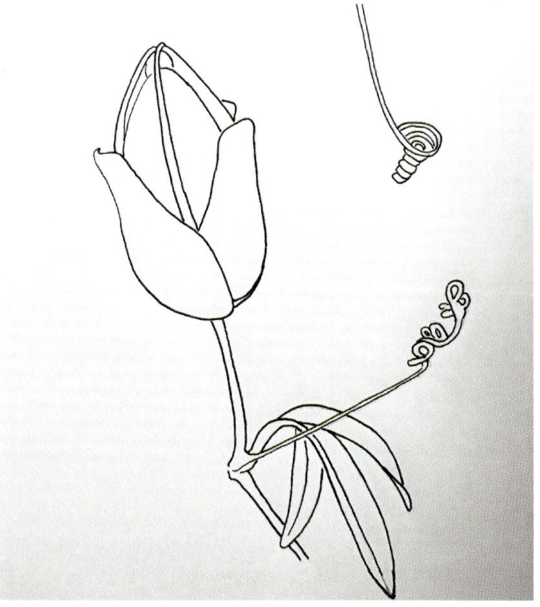

Outline drawing of the stencil design in permanent black ink.

Cutting out the bud design on the acetate using a sharp, pointed Stanley knife.

Areas to be cut out filled in with black, showing white bridges left to hold the stencil together.

Drawing the passion flower bud to use as the design for the second stencil, with bridges in white and areas in black showing where to cut out.

the corners of the stool. Taking photographs of a bud, and the shell once the flower had gone, gave me two more designs of the same plant to work with.

I used the top bud as the reference for my stencil design and first drew it onto a plain white piece of paper. Once I was happy with the outline, I placed a sheet of acetate over the drawing and traced the outline with a permanent drawing pen before blacking out the areas I was going to cut. Using a sharp Stanley knife, I cut out the black areas, making sure that I pulled the Stanley knife towards me while cutting

The cut-out stencil attached to a sample board with masking tape.

and moving the design around to make the cutting easier.

The same process was used for the second bud, with the areas to be cut blacked out as before. The acetate was put on top and held firm with masking tape, and the black areas cut out to form the stencil. The areas in white were left to hold the stencil together.

If the stencil is going to be painted on a flat surface, using masking tape to secure it works well. However, if you are going to stencil on an upright surface, I suggest spraying a light layer of spray mount on the back to hold it firm; it is transparent and makes it easy to lift and move the stencil from place to place. A good trick with spray mount is to wipe it gently across your jeans after you have sprayed the stencil to remove some of the stickiness that you don't want left behind. When you have finished using the stencil, the spray mount can be wiped clean using a soft cloth and white spirit.

I use a very simple method for painting stencils by putting a rag around my forefinger, dipping it in the paint and dabbing it onto the stencil. It is possible to use almost any paint medium for stencilling, and enamel paints are particularly good as they come ready to use with the right consistency, dry quickly and can be cleaned off the stencil so that the stencil can be used many times.

For the passion flower stencilling on this stool, I used gold metal powder mixed with wax, and you can see this process more thoroughly in Chapter 5.

Once one stencil was finished, I cleaned the acetate carefully with a cloth using white spirit, which prevents the paint from building up and making a mess the next time the stencil is used.

The acetate lifted off the stencilled bud.

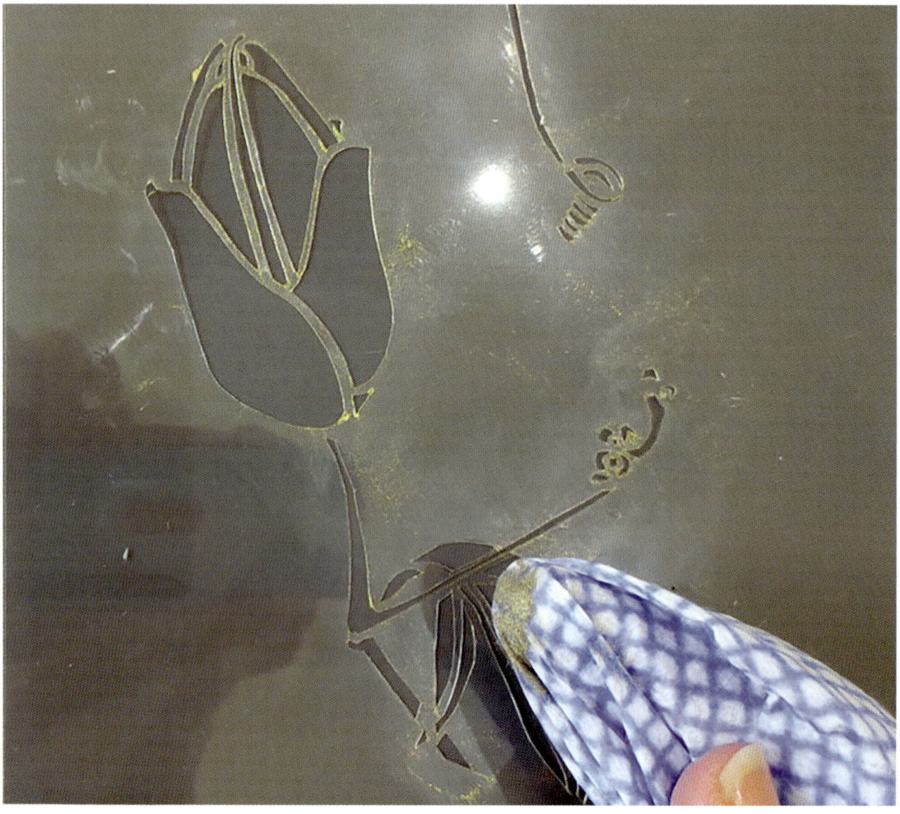

Cleaning the stencil after use. A soft cloth with a little white spirit over your finger and gently wiping the paint from the edges of the stencil works well. You can then use the stencil again without any smudging.

The sample board showing the central and four corner stencils. The corner stencils are flipped so that the tendrils on each bud point to the middle of the design rather than towards the outside edge.

The finished stool showing the stencils painted on the top.

Grapevine Stencil

This stencil is a fun way to liven up a wall or furniture in any setting. If using as a border on a wall it is easy to repeat, and the best way to make sure it stays straight is to measure from the floor to the base of the stencil. This design was based on some fabric that the client wanted to match to, and the petals and grapes were a perfect subject from which to design a stencil. Using the same method as for the stool, I used acetate to make the stencil and then spray mount lightly sprayed onto the reverse to keep the stencil in place.

I painted this stencil as an example on a sample board using artist's oil paints. The materials I needed were artist's oil paints, white spirit, a soft cloth, a palette (I used a plastic lid), a brush for mixing the paints and spray mount. If you prefer, you can use a stencil brush rather than a cloth to dab on the paint – this is the round, stubby brush shown in the photograph.

I used Indian red artist's oil paint and titanium white for the flower petals, grapes and some leaves. I mixed a very small amount of white spirit into the Indian red oil paint. Be careful not to add too much as you don't want it to run. I used a cloth on my finger to dab the paint onto the stencil (although as mentioned, you can use a stencil brush if you prefer). If you use a stencil brush, be sure to keep the brush at right angles to the surface you are stencilling and use a quick hammer motion to get the paint on evenly. I like to use my finger as it gives me more control, adds texture to the work and

The drawing of the grapevine stencil and the cut-out stencil in acetate ready for painting.

Indian red artist's oil paint, mixed with a tiny amount of white spirit and titanium white.

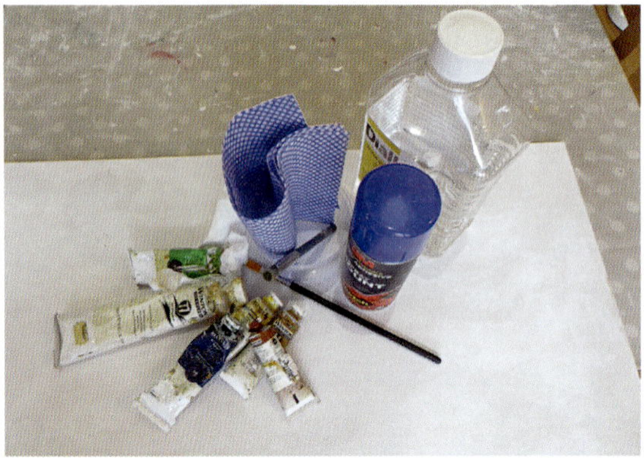

Tools and materials used for stencilling.

With the cloth over my forefinger, I dipped it into a small amount of Indian red oil paint to dab onto the stencil.

Showing the stencil being painted with Indian red paint dabbed onto the petal cut-outs of the stencil.

allows me to move to a clean piece of the cloth quickly and easily. If you use a cloth, make sure to tuck up the area you are not using into your hand, to prevent it getting in the way.

Moving my finger to a clean part of the cloth, I added some undiluted white to the outer edges of the flower petals. With oils, I find it produces a softer finish if colours are added when the paint below is still wet. With enamels, I would wait for the base colour to dry before adding more.

I wanted a two-tone effect on some of the leaves to add movement and depth. The two greens I used were terre verte and permanent sap green. I put the paler terre verte on first and then dabbed a little sap green on the areas I wanted to darken. I used permanent sap green on the main leaf in the middle, using more paint

Using a clean part of the cloth, I added a little white to the Indian red petals on the outer edges.

The leaf on the right-hand side has been filled with terre verte artist's oil paint. The leaf on the left has been filled using terre verte with sap green oil paint on top to darken that area of the leaf.

You can see the difference in tone with the leaf on the right-hand side once sap green has been added, producing a two-tone effect.

Note the darker area on the grape, and the texture left by the cloth, using undiluted Indian red paint.

The finished stencil once the acetate had been removed.

in the centre and slightly less near the edges to give it a light/dark effect.

Adding and building more layers of undiluted paint to areas that you want to darken adds more depth and texture. When you feel that the painting of the stencil is complete, peel the acetate off carefully and remove any residual paint before replacing to paint again.

LETTERING

Design

Typography is a very important part of design and, I must admit, often difficult to get right. I have huge admiration for calligraphers and typographers and when I need to use text I try to keep it simple.

The main things to keep in mind when doing lettering is to try to arrange it so that it is clear and visually in-keeping with the type of design you are painting. If you don't want to create your own font, there are now hundreds to choose from online, and it is worth trying out several before deciding which to use. Some fonts are fatter than others, and therefore take up more space, and some are thinner. The height of the font is also important and I usually print out a couple of options before using one. You need to decide whether to use bold,

A circular table and four rush-seat chairs painted with letters and numbers.

Numbers around the edge of the table painted in burnt sienna as a clock face with the alphabet painted in a circle in lower case and ABC for decoration in the centre.

italic or normal and what colour to choose to complement your artwork.

This table and chair set was a commission through my children's hand-painted furniture online business. The client asked for numbers, capital letters and lower-case letters on the table and on the front and backs of the chairs. Choosing the correct font was important, as it needed to be easy for children to read, plus look fun and clear in both upper and lower case. I chose a classic Times New Roman font and decided to use primary colours with burnt sienna for the numbers in a clock formation around the edge of the table.

Stencils

Stencils are one way to add lettering to your artwork. For this watercolour lion name plate, I chose a French stencil alphabet to paint the name in the centre. The flow and movement of the letters worked well without taking over the painting. I chose a gentle green earth colour for the letters that toned in well with the yellow ochre of the lions. You can pick up interesting stencil alphabets from all over the world, and I keep a stash of them in a drawer. If you find one you like, try to get it in different sizes, as well as in numbers.

Tracing and Painting by Hand

Project – Children's Rush-Seat Chairs

The names on these children's chairs needed to be clear as they are an important part of the whole in personalising the chair for the child. However, I didn't want them to detract from the hand-painted illustrations and so I used a plain font called Arial Rounded MT and left a space between each letter. I printed the names onto a plain sheet of paper and then traced them onto the chair. The colours for the names are a mixture of oil-based white eggshell paint with a little artist's oil paint, diluted with white spirit. I find a calligraphy brush works well for hand-painting lettering and I tipped each chair on its back and painted the letters upside down to avoid touching the painted illustrations on the uprights.

Violet Bookends

I used Times New Roman italic font for the violet bookends discussed in Chapter 1 and chose Payne's grey artist's oil paint to paint the name and date of birth. The violet illustrations are strong, and therefore the colour of the lettering needed to be equally strong, but not so much that it would take over the image. Again, I put a space between each letter.

A lion name plate with the name of the child stencilled using a French-designed stencil in a pale green with ladybirds painted on the letters to add illustration.

Painting the name on the chair using a calligraphy paintbrush and Arial Rounded MT font. The name was traced and painted by hand using a mixture of white oil-based eggshell paint and alizarin crimson artist's oil paint.

This name was painted by hand using a mix of white oil-based eggshell and Prussian blue artist's oil paint.

This name was painted using a mix of white oil-based eggshell and permanent alizarin crimson artist's oil paint.

Violet bookends with the name and date of birth painted in artist's oil paint, Payne's grey. The lettering was traced, and painted by hand using Times New Roman italic font.

Project – Toy Box

In Chapter 7, you will see how the artwork is hand-painted on to this toy box. The name on the lid was painted in white eggshell oil-based paint directly on to the wooden lid. It was important to get the height of the letters right so that the name would not look lost. I decided to use Times New Roman font and printed out the letters on plain white paper first so that I could cut out the letters and place them on the lid, moving them around to get the spacing correct and visually checking that the name looked right. I then traced the letters and attached the tracing to the lid with masking tape.

To make sure that the lid didn't get spoiled with drops or spills of the white oil-based paint, I covered the remainder of the lid with paper.

Letters printed out on white paper using Times New Roman bold font to check that the size and spacing would work on the lid.

Once the spacing and size of lettering was decided, the letters were transferred onto tracing paper to trace onto the lid of the box.

The tracing was then surrounded with paper to avoid any mishaps with paint while the letters were hand-painted.

The toy box with the name painted on the lid with two coats of white oil-based eggshell paint.

After tracing the outline of the letters onto the lid, I painted them with white oil-based paint by hand. As the paint was going directly onto the wood, once the first coat was dry, I painted a second coat so that the letters stood out well.

MDF Letters

Since MDF emerged, it is now possible to get letters made from MDF in all sizes and depths.

They can be fiddly to paint, and it is best to sand the sides with a fine sandpaper before painting. I use the same process as with furniture: two coats of white primer and two coats of either oil-based eggshell or water-based eggshell.

Each of these hand-painted letters measures 18cm (7in) high and so they can stand alone or be attached to a wall, cabinet, door and so on. If you are designing your own letters, it is possible to ask your carpenter to use a font of your choosing.

This bookcase was made of MDF so the surface was ideal for painting and it was decorated using a rag-roll technique in yellow ochre (*see* Chapter 5 for this technique) and then stencilled with small buds using enamel paints.

To decorate the top of this child's desk, I painted the alphabet using Times New Roman font along the edge, using the same colour as the blue on Peter Rabbit's jacket, with Beatrix Potter illustrations in the corners and the centre. I painted the sides of the top of the stool that was to go with the desk with more Beatrix Potter illustrations, leaving the centre empty to sit on.

The letter Q hand-painted with a wildflower illustration of Queen Anne's lace.

The letter S hand-painted with Beatrix Potter illustrations.

The letter A hand-painted with tropical fish illustrations.

Hand-painted wooden letters taken from the Wildflower range on the Sarah Sherrington Designs website.

An MDF bookcase rag-rolled with yellow ochre oil-based scumble glaze, with small bud stencils to add decoration.

The stencil used for decoration on the bookcase.

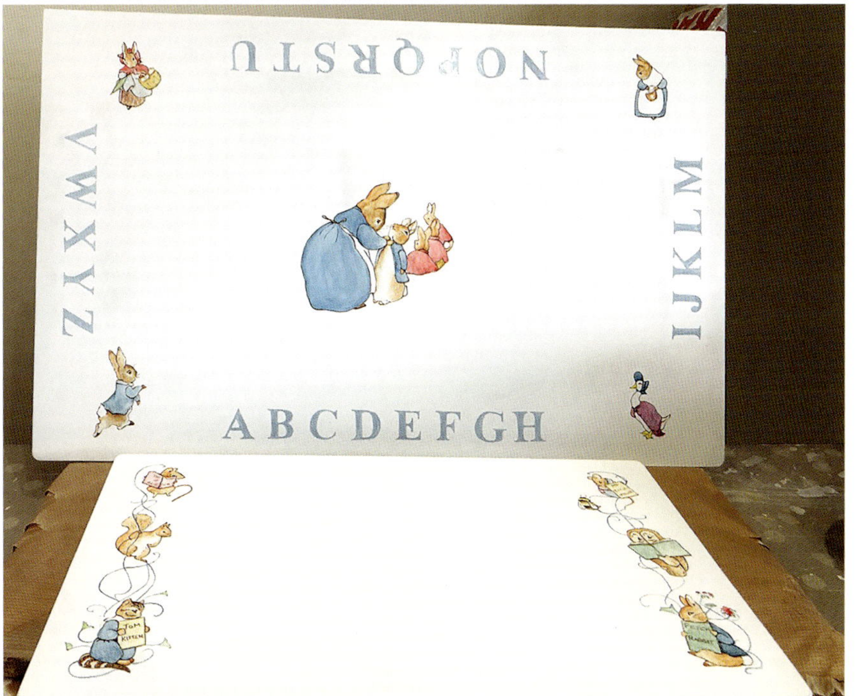

Hand-painted Beatrix Potter desktop and stool. The alphabet is hand-painted along the edge of the desk top using white oil-based eggshell paint mixed with Prussian blue artist's oil paint.

CHAPTER 4

DECOUPAGE AND TRACING

DECOUPAGE

The word decoupage comes from the French word *decouper*, meaning to cut out or cut from something. Decoupage is the art of cutting out images from magazines or other papers and then glueing them to an object before finishing with layers of varnish. It is often combined with special paint effects, such as gold leaf or other decorative elements. It is thought that decoupage originates from East Siberian tomb art, as nomadic tribes decorated tombs with cut felt for decoration. The practice then moved to China, and the ancient Chinese were known for paper cutting, which they used for decorating lanterns and other objects. By the seventeenth century, decoupage had arrived in France as a means for decorating cabinets and pieces of furniture. In Victorian England, decoupage as an art form became very popular, particularly among nobles and royalty. The traditional technique used thirty or more layers of varnish, which were then sanded to a polished finish. A person who does decoupage is known as a *decoupeur*, meaning 'cutter'.

A well-known English decoupage artist from the Georgian era was Mrs Mary Delany. After becoming widowed in her early seventies, and having always been a keen botanist, artist and gardener, she began to decoupage. By using minute pieces of coloured paper, built up in layers, and using the paper to form light and shade, she decoupaged incredibly detailed works incorporating all parts of the plant, often dissecting the piece first to make sure it was accurate. Her work can be seen in the British Museum.

The National Guild of Decoupers was founded in the United States in the 1970s by students of a more contemporary *decoupeur*, Hiram Manning. Hiram Manning discovered the art of decoupage while in Normandy and is known for reviving the art in the United States.

Transfers made of a previous original watercolour of 'honesty', one large central transfer and four smaller ones to be placed in the corners of the table.

Some examples of Mrs Mary Delany's decoupage artworks.

Project – Two-Door Cabinet

To show a form of decoupage that can be very effective, I decided to decoupage a leaf that I had painted as a watercolour on paper onto a reproduction cabinet that needed a bit of a 'lift.' I had painted the cabinet doors with two coats of graphite furniture paint as the background for the leaf (*see* Chapter 2).

I printed out the image on plain paper and carefully cut around the edges. Using PVA glue, I pasted it onto the cabinet door. As you can see, the paper crinkled a bit, but it flattened out as it dried. Mod Podge is another popular glue you can use for decoupage; it is basically a watered-down version of PVA, but you can also get it in spray form. Once the first leaf was in place and drying, I flipped the image and printed out a second leaf for the other door and repeated the process using PVA.

When both leaves were dry, I mixed a little watercolour paint, raw umber, into a water-based clear varnish. I wanted to dull the image a little to make it look less bright but also wanted to keep a natural look. I then painted a coat of tinted varnish onto both door panels, including the graphite background. Leaving the doors to dry for 24 hours, I painted a second coat of tinted varnish.

Watercolour painting of a leaf with a charcoal and watercolour background, which I will photograph and print to make a paper transfer to decoupage the cabinet.

Two coats of graphite water-based furniture paint painted onto the framed squares on the front of the cabinet in Chapter 2.

This shows the leaf printed onto plain white paper and glued onto the cabinet door panel. The crinkles will flatten out when dry.

Clear water-based varnish mixed with raw umber watercolour paint to tint it before brushing onto the door panel.

You can see the difference in tone between the left-hand door, which has just had a coat of tinted varnish, and the right-hand door, which is still unvarnished.

Both cabinet doors with decoupaged leaves once the tinted varnish has dried on both door panels.

Decoupage Using Transfers

Another form of decoupage is to make transfers. Botanical painting is very time consuming and it can take weeks or months to complete a painting, so this is a brilliant way of reproducing your botanical art onto furniture as many times as you like. You can place as many or as few transfers as you wish onto a surface before varnishing. For this small table, I used a watercolour painting I had painted previously of a small sprig of dried 'honesty' (lunaria).

Project – Small Table

There are several transfer papers on the market. I use a waterslide decal paper for inkjet printers. You need to make sure that the transfer paper you buy is the correct one for your printer, either inkjet or laser. Make sure to print your image without using too much ink to avoid bleeding. To do this, select as high a dots per inch (dpi) count as you can and make sure the printer setting is on 'plain paper' and deselect 'high speed'. The image should be printed on the smooth, white, chalky side of the paper. I printed the design five times on the decal paper, one large image for the centre and four smaller versions to place in the corners.

The printed images should be left to dry for at least thirty minutes so that the ink doesn't smudge or run. With a sharp craft knife, cut carefully around the edge of the design, cutting towards you and moving the image around as you go.

Soak one image at a time in a bowl of lukewarm water for about one minute until it is easy to peel the backing sheet off. I keep a pin close by to unfold any parts of the design that fall back on themselves when you lift it. It is a delicate procedure and takes a little practice, especially with small images.

If the piece of furniture you are decoupaging is painted with an oil-based finish, there will be enough glue on the back of your transfer for it to stick. However, if the surface is absorbent, you will need to add more glue. If you are

Watercolour painting of 'honesty' before scanning and printing onto waterslide decal transfer paper.

Cutting out images with sharp pointed Stanley knife.

The small bedside table painted white, ready to be decoupaged.

Leave the image in a bowl of warm water for approximately one minute, which loosens the glue and allows the backing to be peeled away.

The painting printed onto waterslide decal transfer paper, making sure the print is on the chalky white side of the paper.

The backing left in water once the image has been lifted off.

The image gently placed in centre of the table and left to dry.

One central larger image and four smaller ones decoupaged onto tabletop.

transferring your artwork directly onto wood and you want the background to be transparent, paint the wood with real turpentine (white spirit won't work) before placing your transfer. The transfers do not adhere to chalk furniture paint as it is too absorbent, so you would need to seal the paint with varnish first. Place the image carefully on the surface and gently remove any air bubbles by padding it gently using a soft cotton cloth. Once the transfers have dried, seal with two coats of varnish.

Ad Hoc Pieces

Using the same method with the waterslide decal transfer paper, I photographed and then printed a watercolour of a hydrangea that I had painted previously. I use a Canon inkjet printer and so long as the inks are not low, the colours reproduce well. As with the 'honesty' design, once printed, I cut out the image using a sharp Stanley knife and then soaked each piece in a bowl of warm water to remove the backing. I carefully placed both parts of the hydrangea on the already painted grey bedside table I was decorating, and when the transfers were dry, I sealed them with two coats of water-based varnish. It is important not to varnish too soon, as the transfers can take longer than you think to dry; I usually leave them over night to be sure. If they are not properly dry, the varnish can wipe out some of the colour and detail. The base paint previously used on this bedside table was a silk paint and non-absorbent.

To keep for a later date, I also scanned a watercolour painting of ash leaves before the original watercolour painting was complete; I could then use this scan for printed transfers. This was because I intended to paint the background of the original watercolour black, and I wanted a transfer of the leaves while they were looking slightly washed out that I could use directly on wood, rather than on a painted piece of furniture. As mentioned before, the wood must be painted with real turpentine before decorating with these transfers.

My watercolour painting of a hydrangea printed onto decal waterslide transfer paper.

The hydrangea transfer has been cut out with a Stanley knife, and is soaking in a bowl of lukewarm water to soften the glue before removing the backing.

Once you have removed the backing, carefully place on the piece of furniture and dab gently with a soft cotton cloth to remove any air bubbles.

The hydrangea transfers in place on the surface of the bedside table and varnished with two coats of water-based clear varnish.

Project – Chair

To decorate this small painted white chair with a wooden seat, I decided to decoupage using torn images of flowers and plants from a gardening magazine. This is a fun way to decoupage, and you really can't go wrong. It is best to tear the pictures out of the magazine, as using scissors or a knife leaves hard edges, whereas the soft torn edges blend well from one to another.

A watercolour painting of ash leaves before the painting was finished.

A set of four ash leaf transfers printed on waterslide decal transfer paper to keep for a later date.

The original watercolour painting of ash leaves once finished with a painted charcoal and watercolour background.

First, I checked that I had torn out enough pieces to cover the area. It is best to have too many as it becomes a bit of a random jigsaw, and you will need to overlap in some places. I used PVA, and mixed two-thirds glue and one-third water. Adding a little water makes the glue smoother and creamier to use.

A fitch brush is a good brush to use if you have some edges that haven't stuck, as the straight edge of the fitch is easy to slip under the edges with additional glue. Before varnishing your decoupage, check that all the pieces are glued flat; you may need to add a little more glue to make sure.

Around the edge of the chair seat there were gaps in my jigsaw of tear-outs, and so I tore some small pieces of greenery to fill them in. Once all the glue was dry, I varnished the seat with two coats of water-based satin varnish before sanding gently with very fine wet and dry sandpaper. After wiping the area clean from any dust, I added another coat of water-based varnish. Make sure each coat of varnish you put on is completely dry before adding the next.

The white-painted child's chair ready to be decoupaged with botanical pictures torn from a gardening magazine.

All you need for this type of decoupage is PVA glue and a small paintbrush. I used a fitch and I diluted the PVA with a little water in a small plastic bowl.

Brushing the PVA mixture onto the back of each torn-out flower, I glued them onto the seat of the chair.

To prevent gaps around the edge of the chair, I filled any holes with torn pieces of greenery from the magazine. Once dry, I varnished it with three coats of water-based satin varnish. You need to leave at least one hour for the varnish to dry between coats.

The decoupaged child's chair.

TRACING

Tracing is a way of copying designs from one place to another using a translucent paper.

In the 1390s, Cennino d'Andrea Cennini wrote a technical guide to help his art students with various methods of making tracing paper (*carta da lucido*). One method was to get some fish glue and leaf glue, which was available in chemists at the time, and soak six leaves in a small bowl and boil until it melted. When the mixture was still warm, it needed to be strained before being brushed onto smooth slabs of marble or porphyry (the stone slabs needed be clean and greased with olive oil beforehand). This was then left to dry before being prised off the stone with the point of a sharp knife, while trying not to damage it. To make it more durable, before prying off the stone it could be coated with linseed oil and left to dry for two or three more days.

Cennino d'Andrea Cennini's second method was to scrape kid parchment until it only just held together, with as even a finish as possible, until it became transparent. It could then be smeared with fine linseed oil using a cotton cloth and left for several days to dry.

The final method suggested in his technical guide was to make tracing paper from very thin paper, which became transparent after being greased several times with linseed oil and left to dry.

The versatility of tracing paper means that it can be used for most drawing media, fine line drawings and overlays. Historically it was used for work plans by architects and engineers as well as artists. Mass-produced tracing paper dates from about 1820, soon after machine-made paper began to be produced.

Tracing paper is an excellent way to transfer your designs before painting onto furniture. For example, in Chapter 3, you saw an example of letters being transferred onto furniture before painting. You can also move a tracing around and draw on both sides to use the image in different directions – *see*, for example, the hand-painted toy box later in this chapter.

A light box is a great tool for tracing. The screen has a bright backlight that shines through the image you put on the light box so that you can trace the same image again onto a clean sheet of paper. As an example of its usefulness, I had mistakenly managed to spatter red pigment onto a sketch I had drawn of a dried peony; I wanted to redraw the image without starting all over again. I placed the spattered drawing onto the light box and placed a clean sheet of paper over the top to trace onto.

A drawing of the peony on a light box ready to trace.

The light shines behind the original image, and a plain piece of drawing paper is put over the top to trace the new peony.

Project – Tulip Wastepaper Basket

Computers are also very helpful tools for tracing. For example, I uploaded a photograph of the nigella-African-bride seed heads taken on a black background (Chapter 1) onto an old monitor and placed a plain white sheet of baking paper over the image. I traced around the outline of the seed heads in preparation for using the drawing on the front of the tulip wastepaper basket project. I often use non-stick baking paper for tracing as it comes on a roll, which makes it easier to trace large images or cut to the size I need.

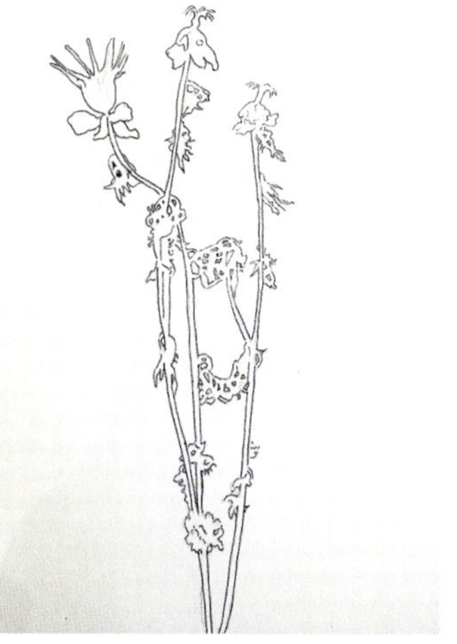

The outline of the nigella-African-bride seed heads in black pen.

A computer monitor with a photograph of nigella-African-bride seed heads loaded on the screen for tracing.

I attached a sheet of white baking paper over the monitor to trace the outline of the image.

Project – Coffee Table

For the faux wood coffee table, I chose a dried sprig of bay leaves for the central design. Having drawn the image I wanted to reproduce, I traced it onto the table using a baking sheet, so that I could clearly see the outline of what I was later going to hand-paint. When pencilling over the lines on the back of the tracing sheet, use a soft lead but not too dark. You don't want excess lead on the piece you are about to paint as it will smudge into the artwork. *See* Chapters 6 and 7 for the next steps in this project.

The tracing of bay leaves in the centre square of the faux wood coffee table, held in place with pieces of masking tape.

Project – Toy Box

For the hand-painted toy box, I traced the daisies to paint on the sides of the toy box. Once I had pencilled all the daisies on the back of the tracing, I attached the tracing paper to the toy box with masking tape to keep it in place. I also traced the poppy image and rowan berry images on the same toy box. Use a sharp pencil to shade over the lines of the daisies so that the pencil you have put on the reverse side comes through. Once you have the outlines, it is time to add some colour (*see* Chapter 7).

Project – Children's Rush-Seat Chairs

The area to paint on the rush-seat chairs is only 2cm (3/4in) wide on each side, so in a case like this you need to plan and measure your design carefully. Here you can see the sketch and tracings before transferring the outline and painting the poppies onto Poppy's chair. *See* Chapter 7 for the painting process.

Project – Bedside Cabinet

To hand-paint the blackberries on the top of a bedside cabinet (*see* Chapter 7 for the painting process), I traced the blackberries with reference from a photograph to make sure that the size and the scale of the painting would fit neatly onto the surface.

Project – Two-Drawer Chest

I used the same method as the bedside cabinet for the two-drawer chest that I decided to paint a larger-than-life peony on. Using a photograph from my library, I enlarged it and then traced it to give an outline for the painting.

A tracing of the outline of the poppies for the centre front panel of the toy box.

Tracings of daisies to put on the sides of the toy box. The tracings were reversed and traced again on the opposite side of the toy box.

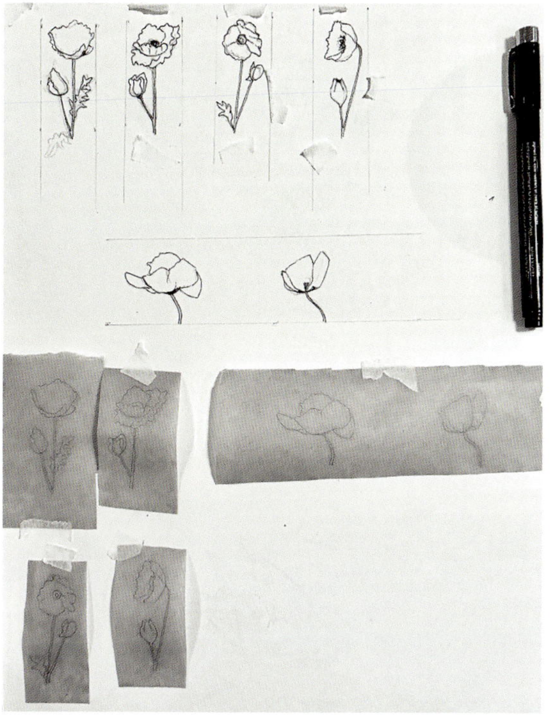

Sketches and tracings of poppies to paint on a child's rush-seat chair. The maximum width available to paint the designs is 2.5cm (1in), so it is important to draw them to the correct size beforehand.

Once I had traced the poppy outlines onto the chair, I then painted them using artist's oil paints.

A photograph of a blown peony to use as reference for an image to be painted on the surface of a wooden two-drawer chest.

The tracing to be used to hand-paint blackberries onto the top of a bedside cabinet.

Tracings of the peony ready to place on the two-drawer chest for painting.

CHAPTER 5

METAL POWDERS

Gold leaf was originally beaten by hand to produce powders. In the twelfth century it became clear that the same method for making gold powders worked equally well for other metals. In about 1840, Bessemer, from Nuremburg in Germany, which was already well known for its brass industry, invented a mechanised process for making bronze powders at much cheaper prices. This resulted in bronze powders being more economical and accessible around the world.

Bronze powders are often used in place of gold leaf, which can still be prohibitively expensive. The metal powders are intended to resemble the many different colours of gold and bronze and are often used by gilders in repairing picture frames and pieces of furniture. Bronze powders are made up of mixes of copper and zinc and can tarnish over time if not protected. When the powder is mixed with gilt wax, the finish is non-tarnishing and can be buffed to a shine with a soft cloth. The colour may fade slightly over time, so it is a good idea to finish with a varnish or lacquer.

A stencil of a passion flower bud painted with bronze powders, old gold.

PROJECT – STOOL

I wanted to use metal powders to decorate an old stool. Using a large sheet of plyboard as a sample board, I used the same paints that I used to prepare the stool (*see* Chapter 2), as I wanted to see how the composition and bronze powders would look before doing the real thing.

I used Superfine Metallic Bronze Powder (Gold 2.5) and mixed a small teaspoon of this powder with a small teaspoon of gilt wax

Tools and materials used for the metal powder artwork on the stool: pot of gilt wax medium; pot of Superfine Metallic Bronze Powder in gold; ceramic eggcup/palette; teaspoon.

A stencilled bud on the sample board showing a two-tone effect using gold metal powder with bronze metal powder used for shading.

The sample board showing the stencilled design using gold metal powder mixed with gilt wax medium.

The gilt wax medium on a spoon to be mixed with Superfine Metallic Bronze Powder in gold.

The paste-like consistency of the gilt wax medium mixed with Roberson Superfine Metallic Bronze Powder (Gold 2.5).

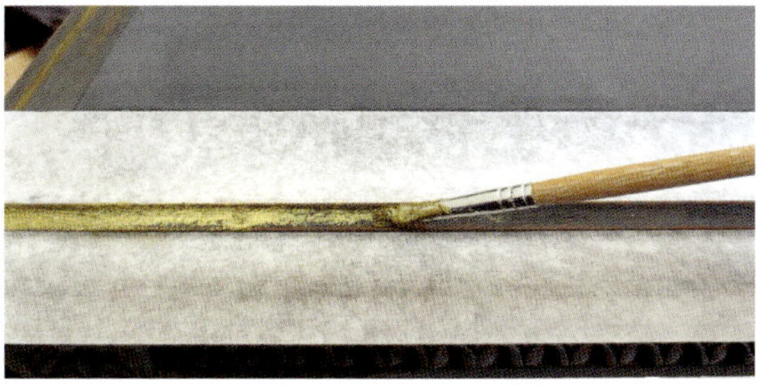

With masking tape covering above and below the line to be painted, I used a small flat-tipped brush with strong bristles.

The line once the masking tape has been removed. Try to pull off the masking tape as soon as possible after painting, as it helps with leaving clean edges.

medium. Getting the consistency right takes a bit of trial and error, so I suggest testing a small amount of both in a cup first. I used a ceramic egg cup, which proved ideal as it also had a cut-out for a spoon alongside, so I could mix all I needed on one palette.

The process of stencilling onto the sample board is shown in Chapter 3. I painted up two squares on the sample board in graphite, so that I could choose between two different effects with the stencils. On one square, I added Roberson Superfine Metallic Bronze Powder (Gold 2.5) mixed with a little gilt wax medium. On the other, I used the Roberson Superfine Metallic Bronze Powder (Old Bronze) metal powder on top of the gold to get a two-tone effect. However, once I compared the two, I preferred the stencilled effect on the plain gold side of the sample board.

Once I was happy with the composition and colouring on the sample board, I was ready to stencil the same layout on the top of the stool (*see* Chapter 3). Before stencilling the top, I wanted to smarten up the edges and form a frame around the top of the stool with gold lines. Placing masking tape above and below the areas to be painted, to avoid the gold mix spilling onto the wrong area, I used the same mix of Roberson Superfine Metallic Bronze Powder (Gold 2.5) and gilt wax to paint the lines.

Using the same gold mix, I then picked out the details that were on the legs and corners of the stool, before adding the stencilled design on the top.

I then buffed up the gold with a soft cloth and varnished the stool, as it is to be used as a bedside table and a protective layer was necessary.

Detail on the stool picked out with gold. You can also see the gold stencilling on the top.

More detail beginning to be picked out; I used a small brush to cover the circles.

The finished stool once varnished and polished, with the gold areas buffed up with a soft cloth.

PROJECT – CHEST OF DRAWERS

Upcycling an old and tattered cornflower blue chest of drawers passed through various stages before framing the top (*see* Chapters 1, 2, 6 and 7). Once these stages had been completed, I wanted to hold it all together with a fine frame around the top using Roberson Superfine Metallic Bronze Powder (Old Bronze), as it seemed the perfect colour combination with the poppy seed heads and distressed paintwork.

I mixed a little of the old bronze metallic powder with gilt wax medium to form a paste in a ceramic eggcup and then, to keep a clean line, I masked off the area I was going to paint.

Using a small fitch brush, I painted the bronze metallic paste along the line and then wiped it gently with stockinette on my forefinger. I wanted to have a good metallic bronze look but I also wanted it to tone in well with the poppy seed heads, and so distressed it slightly by wiping it off so that it wasn't too solid. Stockinette is available to buy in most garages and DIY stores. It is bought in a large roll and it is cotton. When you cut off a length from the roll, fold the edges into the centre of the pad so that fragments of cotton don't stray into the paint.

Although it was only a narrow bronze line, the medium worked well in bonding the poppy seed heads and the distressed paint finish on the chest of drawers together.

Bronze powder and gilt wax medium.

Mixing bronze powder and gilt wax medium together in preparation for painting.

Masking the top of the chest of drawers before painting a line in bronze powder.

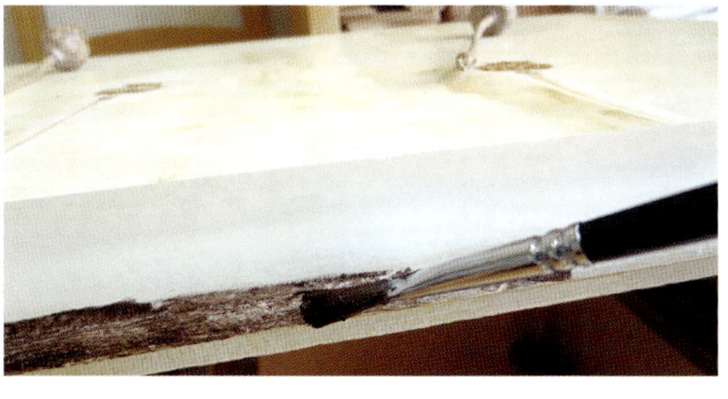
Using a small fitch with strong bristles to paint a line along the top edge of the chest of drawers; the masking tape helps to keep the line sharp.

The finished line painted in bronze powder and gilt wax medium along the top edge of the chest of drawers.

PROJECT – TWO-DRAWER CHEST

The handles on the two-drawer chest were either broken or missing, and so I decided to replace them with 44mm unfinished pine wooden knobs painted in a faux lapis lazuli. It meant filling one hole in each place where the original handles had been before painting the chest.

Chapter 6 shows a small sample board painted with lapis lazuli. The final part of painting the lapis lazuli is to gently flick some bronze powders onto the wet surface to imitate the glint that you would get from looking at the original stone. I flicked a little of each bronze powder, in gold and bronze, on each knob and then let them dry. Once they were dry, I painted a thin line of bronze powder mixed with a little gilt wax medium around each of the knobs.

The wooden two-drawer chest needed four holes filled where the old handles had been. The green circles show the position of the holes that were filled.

Using a small, pointed brush to paint a gold line around the knob, using a mix of bronze powder (gold) and gilt wax medium. There was not enough space to mask off above and below the line, so it was painted very carefully without.

A small sample board of painted lapis lazuli being flicked with bronze powders once the painted detail was finished.

The pine knob before painting and after painting.

PROJECT – BRONZE POWDER WITH GLAZE

It is also possible to mix bronze powders with glaze to produce a luxurious effect. To demonstrate this, I painted a sample board with flat black matt paint and sanded it with no. 600 wet and dry sandpaper to make sure it was as smooth as possible. I then mixed some gold bronze powder into the water-based glaze and stirred, adding a very small amount of water, to create the consistency of single cream.

A sample board painted with graphite water-based paint, sanded with wet and dry sandpaper no. 600 to a very fine finish.

Bronze powder (gold) mixed with water-based glaze to the consistency of single cream. There is also a pad of stockinette to use in a rag-roll effect.

I brushed the mixed gold glaze onto the surface with a brush, ensuring not to spread the glaze too thinly. Next, I cut a length of stockinette and folded the edges up into the middle to make a pad. Then, with a firm pressure, I rolled this over the painted area to move the glaze. Little bits of cotton from the stockinette that stray from the pad can easily be removed later when the effect has dried.

The result will be a luxurious undulating, leaf-like effect, and when it has dried and been buffed up with a soft cloth, it is a great effect for decoration on small areas on painted furniture.

Painting glaze onto the sample board.

Glaze painted onto sample board quite thickly.

Using a pad of stockinette, rag-rolling firmly to remove glaze.

A gold leafy effect on the sample board left to dry before buffing with a soft cloth and removing any bits of cloth left behind.

PROJECT – BRONZE POWDER WITH ENAMEL

To paint a faux lacquer effect, I firstly made sure that the area on the sample board was clean from dust and sanded with the highest grade sandpaper, making sure that the surface was as smooth as possible. I then painted on a coat of black enamel paint, using a soft wide fitch brush preventing the brush strokes from showing while leaving a gloss shine.

While the enamel was still wet, I flicked bronze powder (gold) and bronze powder (bronze) onto the surface. Dipping the tip of the brush in the powder and then holding it high above the board while tapping it against the wooden handle of another brush to let the powder fall onto the enamel. To obtain a bit of movement, I blew the powder across the board, especially where more had dropped in one place than another.

This is a lovely effect to paint on small areas or items, and an example of this is the faux lacquer painted on this wooden knob.

Black enamel paint painted onto sample board with a wide, soft fitch. The painted square is masked off with masking tape to keep the edges clean and straight.

Dipping the ends of the brush into bronze powder (gold) and flicking it on enamel paint when wet.

The bronze and gold powder blown from left to right across the sample board and left to dry.

A wooden knob painted with black enamel paint.

The same technique is used as with the sample board to flick bronze powders onto the wet enamel paint on the knob.

CHAPTER 6

DECORATIVE TECHNIQUES

The origin of decorative painting goes back 15,000–20,000 years to the earliest cave paintings where mixtures of ochres, charcoal and animal fat were used, and successive calcite flows have preserved these paintings in a remarkable way. This claims to be the origin of the profession 'decorative painter'. The wide variety of earth colours have been the basis of techniques that have barely changed. Around 2000BC, tufts of animal hair were inserted into bamboo sticks by the Chinese, making the first paintbrush that we know of.

Following cave paintings, 'fresco' emerged in approximately 1800BC, starting in Mesopotamia and then in Egypt due to the creation of lime kilns. Many figurative representations and even fake marble were found in tombs in Egypt; this was followed by the Greeks who used marbling on columns and buildings to enhance them. The Romans used fresco in a more decorative way, but after a decline during the fall of the Roman Empire, decorative painting was lost until the Italian Renaissance, where decorative painting sprang up again in churches, palaces and on monuments. The profession of a decorative painter became official in 1258, by bringing together corporations of painters who were commissioned to paint the walls of churches, reproducing biblical illustrations, and to embellish the architecture.

The evolution and influence of decorative techniques using oil paint, now available in tubes, was neck and neck with England and France, before spreading throughout Europe. In 1882, the Institut superieur de la peinture decorative Van Der Kelen in Belgium opened as the first school to teach the profession of decorative techniques such as the imitation of fake wood, fake marble and other various materials.

The painting of the decorative technique porphyry painted onto the back upright of a bedside cabinet with bright decorative hand-painted blackberries on the top.

PROJECT – TULIP WASTEPAPER BASKET

As mentioned in Chapter 1, I wanted the wastepaper basket to have a very dark background similar to mahogany so that the nigella-African-bride seed heads would stand out as the final decoration. You can see the preparation for the bin in Chapter 2, where it was painted with the first coats ready for the decorative technique to be applied.

I decided not to use a scumble glaze for the paint effect as I wanted to build up layers with as great a depth of colour as possible. Once scumble glaze is used, you cannot add more coats on the top as it removes the glaze below. When painting a faux mahogany effect, the ideal base colour to use is orange, and so for this paint effect I mixed together some orange oil-based eggshell, burnt umber artist's oil paint and brilliant red artist's oil paint with white spirit. The eggshell worked well to thicken the mixture, but you should be careful not to use too much or it will become sticky and difficult to use. I added more white spirit than I would normally use to mix a colour so that it was slightly runnier than single cream.

Once I had brushed on the first layer, I wanted to remove the brush strokes. Using a pad of stockinette, I gently dabbed the paint all over; this removed the brush strokes and gave it a gentle mottled effect. I then let it dry for 24 hours.

Materials for the base coats: pale orange oil-based eggshell and a paint tray with brilliant red and burnt umber artist's oil paint.

The first coat brushed onto the white background, a mix of pale orange eggshell, burnt umber and brilliant red artist's oil paint.

The first coloured coat has been painted and the brush strokes removed by gently padding the surface with a pad of stockinette.

The seed head decoration would be painted onto the front of the bin. I didn't want the artwork to sit on top of the finished background, so I needed to make sure that I left the area clear of the very dark finish by creating a template to mask the area off. While the paint was drying on the bin, I traced the outline of the seed head decoration onto a sheet of medium surface cartridge pad; this paper was neither too thick nor too thin to use as a template. Using a sharp Stanley knife, I cut out a rough outline of the template.

To make sure that the cut-out didn't move while I painted on the second layer of dark paint, I attached it with small pieces of masking tape in different places. I used the previous mixture of pale orange eggshell and burnt umber and brilliant red artist's oil paints and loosely brushed it onto the bin and over the attached seed head cut-out. I then brushed into the wet paint strips of burnt umber and brilliant red.

Using a pad of stockinette, I carefully blotted the area I had just painted and then using a badger brush, I softened the brush marks to blend the colours together. The badger brush is, as the name suggests, made from very soft badger hair and the technique is to quickly move it up, down, right and left with the tip of the bristles hardly touching the paint. After softening the brush strokes, I carefully lifted the seed head cut-out off the bin. The result looks messy but leaves a pale area in the right shape in which to later paint the seed heads.

Once the background was dry enough, I began to address the messy area where the seed heads would be painted. I liked the fact that there were shadows and some subtle colouring left by the first layer of paint. Using a small brush and white oil-based eggshell, mixed with

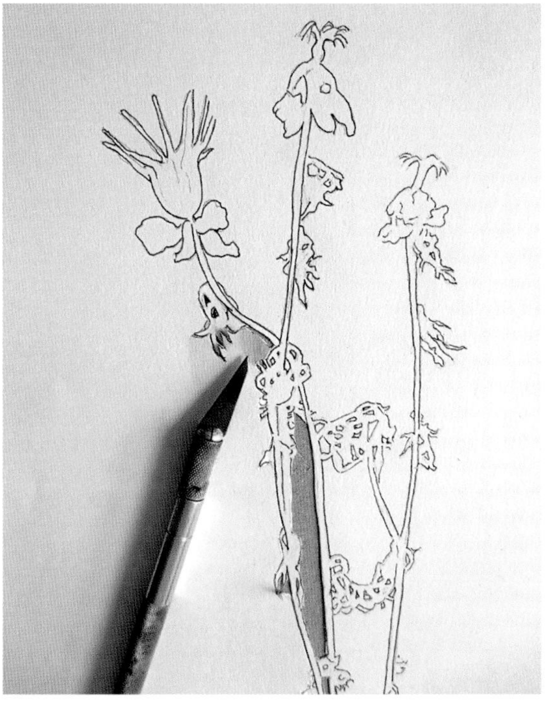

Placing the drawing on a thick sheet of card, I roughly cut around the outline of the seed head illustration using a sharp Stanley knife.

The cut-out of the template for nigella-African-bride seed heads. It is quite roughly done, but enough to block out the next dark coat to be painted on the bin.

The cut-out was attached to the bin using small pieces of masking tape to keep it in place.

The original paint mix is painted all over the sides of the bin and over the cut-out. I then used the same brush with burnt umber and brilliant red artist's oil paint to add strips of the two colours onto the other sides of the bin.

A badger brush is used to soften the brush marks.

a little white spirit, I carefully started to fill the area left by the template.

The spindly tendrils looked a little clunky with the white paint, so I waited until it was dry and then used artist's burnt umber oil paint with a little white spirit to paint in between the tendrils, enabling me to narrow areas where necessary. The technical

When the cut-out is lifted off it leaves behind a pale area in which to paint the seed heads later.

A side of the bin without the cut-out where the colours have been softened with stockinette and with the badger brush.

Beginning to paint some detail on the seed heads, using white oil-based eggshell paint with white spirit. Painting carefully around the tendrils using burnt umber artist's oil paint for definition.

term for painting this way is using 'negative space', simply put, using the area around and between a subject.

I wanted the background to look darker still, so that the seed heads would stand out more. I used the original mixture of pale orange oil-based eggshell, artist's burnt umber oil paint, artist's brilliant red oil paint and white spirit. I had kept the original mixture in a jar with the lid screwed on, so that the colour mix didn't change. For this layer, I did not need to use stockinette or the badger brush to soften the brush strokes.

Another coat of paint to darken the background further.

Showing the rich mahogany colour on two sides of the bin.

FAUX CARRARA MARBLE

Carrara marble, known as Luna marble to the Romans, is very popular for use in interiors. It is found in the mountains outside the city of Carrara in northern Italy. Originally it was a pure white stone and used for sculpting monuments. It lent itself well to polishing and it was strong enough to achieve very fine detail. Some examples of monuments sculpted from Carrara marble include Marble Arch and the Victoria Memorial in London. However, by the late twentieth century, the pure white marble had been excavated to oblivion and the Carrara marble now quarried in Carrara has a slightly greyish tint with streaks of black and grey on white. It is still a very popular marble, particularly for tiles and interiors.

This decorative paint effect works well using either a water-based glaze or an oil-based glaze. The obvious advantages for the water-based glaze are that it dries quickly and is odourless. The oil-based glaze has a strong smell and takes a day or two to dry. Should you make a mistake using the water-based glaze, it is easy to wipe off with water on a soft cloth. When using oil-based glaze, the same applies but with white spirit on a soft cloth.

I used a sample board to demonstrate the painted Carrara marble effect using water-based paint and glaze on one side and oil-based paint and glaze on the other. You will need to prepare the piece you are painting as in Chapter 2, using either two coats of water-based eggshell or two coats of oil-based eggshell as the base, after painting your primer, depending on your preference.

Tools and materials for the Carrara marble effect using water-based scumble glaze and paints: a goose feather for veins, stockinette, artist's watercolour paints, a badger brush and a decorator's paint brush.

Tools and materials for the Carrara marble effect using oil-based scumble glaze and paints: stockinette, artist's oil paints, a badger brush, white spirit and a decorator's brush.

A sample board with water-based eggshell paint on the left and oil-based eggshell paint on right.

For the example described here, I used a water-based scumble glaze, but it is exactly the same process if you use an oil-based scumble glaze. Once the base coats were dry, I put some water-based scumble glaze into a paint bucket and on a separate plate I mixed some black artist's watercolour paint with a bit of water; I then added this to the glaze and stirred it in. I kept some of the black paint mixed with a little water aside as I would need it later. I added some yellow ochre and then some white. When all mixed together, it should be the colour of putty. It is important to ensure that the glaze doesn't become too watery – it should be the consistency of single cream.

The mix of colours to use for the Carrara marble effect: white, black, yellow ochre and a mix of white and black for a dark grey. The same colours for either the water-based or oil-based Carrara marble effect apply.

Glaze, the colour of putty, painted onto the sample board using a decorator's paintbrush with the strokes going in one direction.

Dip your brush into the black mixed paint on your palette, and brush it onto the glaze going in the same direction as before, leaving space in between each shadow you paint.

Dip the tip of the goose feather, or small fitch brush, into the dark grey paint mix on your palette and add jagged vein lines over the shadows going in the same direction of the previous brush strokes.

Using a decorator's brush, I painted the glaze onto the surface, pulling the brush to the side so that all brush marks go in one direction.

I then put a little of the previously mixed black on the brush and create darker areas, like shadows, with the brush still going in the same direction.

I worked quite quickly to ensure the glaze stayed wet and didn't become tacky. Next, I took the goose feather (you can also use a small fitch brush, but I prefer the bendiness of goose feathers) and dipped the pointed feather end into the dark grey mix of paint on the palette. I worked the tip of the brush along the shadowy areas I had painted to form veins, keeping them thin and jagged and going in the same direction as before. A good tip is to hold the feather in your left hand if you are right-handed, and if you are left-handed, hold it in your right hand, so that the result doesn't look too controlled.

Next, I cut a length of stockinette from the roll and folded the cut edges, which tend to fray, into the centre (this prevents any bits and pieces getting into the wet glaze). With the pad of stockinette, I gently but firmly padded the painting all over to remove the brush marks.

To remove brush strokes, pad firmly all over using a pad of stockinette.

A badger brush is a must-have for decorative paint effects. Made, as mentioned earlier in this chapter, with pure badger hair, it is beautifully soft and comes in small or large sizes. I treasure my badger brushes, not just because they are expensive but also because you cannot complete many paint effects without one. I keep them very clean and often wash them with baby shampoo to keep the softness. I held the badger brush upright above the painting and, only just touching the paint, kept my wrist and the badger brush moving quickly in different directions, to soften the whole piece.

Dipping the tip of the goose feather into the dark grey mixed paint on my palette and, using the same technique as I did previously, I built up the veins where they were before. I used jagged motions, adding a few more veins where necessary and changing the weight on the feather to get thick and thin lines. Then I badgered the area I was painting again and left it to dry.

The sample board now shows the marbling painted on both sides, one side using a water-based glaze, and the other an oil-based glaze. There is a difference of colour simply because I added more yellow ochre to one mix than to the other, but otherwise there is very little difference between the two.

Holding the badger brush upright, soften the area you are painting with quick movements in all directions.

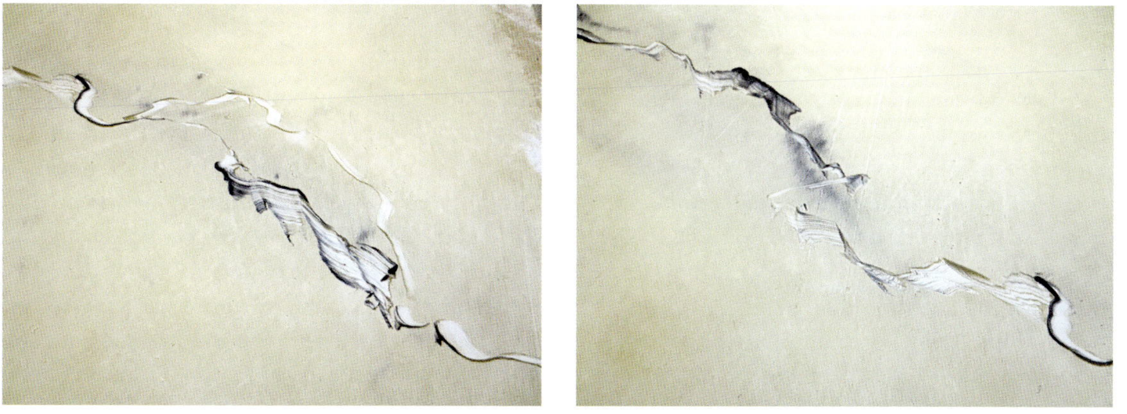

Final veins painted with the dark grey mix, showing what is achieved by changing the weight and jagged line as you go.

The sample board showing Carrara marble painted using water-based glaze on the left-hand side and oil-based glaze on the right-hand side.

Project – Garden Coffee Table

To paint this small, round coffee table, after two coats of primer I sprayed it with racing green spray paint. I left a circle in the centre of the tabletop and painted it in with two coats of white water-based eggshell in preparation for painting faux Carrara marble using water-based glaze. To neaten the circle edge between the green paint and the marble, I hand-painted a narrow line using raw umber artist's oil paint. As you will see in Chapter 7, I painted clumps of flower petals to decorate the green area of the tabletop using a Chinese paintbrush.

A garden coffee table painted with faux Carrara marble in a circle in the centre of the table, using water-based glaze and artist's watercolours, following the same technique as used on the sample board.

FAUX PORPHYRY

Porphyry is a very hard purple-coloured stone with pieces of quartz shining through the purple. Its name comes from ancient Greek, meaning 'purple'. In the early fourth and fifth centuries it was found in a quarry in the Eastern Desert of Egypt and, being an incredibly hard stone, was used for building projects and monuments. Due to the colour purple being synonymous with royalty, it was known as 'imperial porphyry'; being a very rare stone, for Roman emperors it became a prestigious statement of importance with which to build sarcophaguses and monuments.

After the fifth century, the red porphyry quarry was lost due to troubles in Egypt at that time. It wasn't discovered again until 1823 by an English Egyptologist when the Eastern Desert was reopened for study.

If you wish to see an example of porphyry in the UK, the sarcophagus of Arthur Wellesley, the First Duke of Wellington, can be found in St Paul's Cathedral, London. It was completed in 1858 and is built from a single sheet of a type of porphyry called luxullianite that was surprisingly found in a field in Cornwall.

A roll of stockinette, fitch brushes and two sizes of badger brush to use for painting faux porphyry.

Project – Bedside Cabinet

I mixed white oil-based eggshell paint and some artist's alizarin crimson to make a pale pink base coat before painting the porphyry effect. For this painting, I decided to use oil-based paints and glaze as I think it provides more depth with this paint effect. Water-based paints dry very quickly, as it doesn't take long for the water to evaporate; by contrast, oil paints are required to oxidise and therefore the drying time is longer.

The colours used to paint faux porphyry are alizarin crimson, burnt sienna and ultramarine. The crimson is transparent, and so only a little glaze should be used. I mixed the crimson first with a tiny bit of glaze, then added burnt sienna to add body to the mix; I then added some ultramarine until the mixture was a rich blackcurrant colour. If there is too much glaze,

A mixture of white eggshell paint with artist's alizarin crimson to make a pale pink base coat for the porphyry.

it will appear very thin when painted so you may have to do a couple of trials to get it right. If you think your first attempt is too thin, it is easily wiped off with a soft cloth and white spirit. I brushed the blackcurrant mix of paint and glaze onto the sample board and then removed the brush strokes with a pad of stockinette.

I then softened all over using the badger brush at right angles to the paint, moving it quickly in different directions. I mixed some alizarin crimson and ultramarine with white spirit to make a very dark colour to the consistency of ink and, using my fitch brush, spattered the painting. To spatter, I held the fitch against a piece of wood (you could also hold it against a large brush) above the painting and tapped. I then cleaned my brush and, with a little white spirit, mixed titanium white and alizarin crimson to the same consistency as before and spattered the piece again.

I painted faux porphyry on the bedside cabinet project, adding hand-painted blackberries to the top in Chapter 7. The colour and style of porphyry suited the artwork, and vice versa.

Alizarin crimson, ultramarine and burnt sienna artist's oil paint mixed in a paint bucket. A square of the mix, painted and padded with stockinette, on a sample board.

A sample square to be softened with a badger brush.

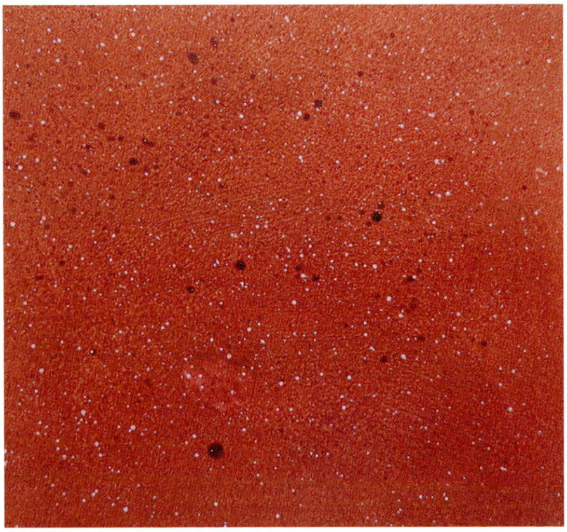

A square of faux porphyry painted on the sample board.

A porphyry-stone-effect cabinet with blackberries.

FAUX WOOD EFFECT

Wood-graining became popular in England towards the end of the seventeenth century, probably due to the Great Fire of London in 1666. The quantity of oak needed to rebuild the city was too much for the stock available and so fixtures began to be made from pine. This cheaper wood was cleverly disguised as oak by using wood-graining techniques. Even without the Great Fire of London, the age of oak was on the wane and decorative walnut furniture was becoming popular. Panelling, which had always been made in oak, was instead being made with pine or lime and painted. The quality of graining was fairly basic, improving greatly by the 1850s, and today techniques can be so sophisticated that it can be difficult to see the difference between the original and the painted.

The illusion of wood-graining in the home can be a realistic version of a certain type of wood, or a fantasy wood created using the imagination. Contrasting different types of wood on one piece can create strength and character.

Project – Coffee Table

For this coffee table, I used my imagination and painted a type of wood grain that suited the room it would be placed in, both in colour and character. Inserting a frame of tortoiseshell and a contrasting marquetry inner frame gave the tabletop decoration, as well as strength.

Once the filling, sanding and base coats had been completed (*see* Chapter 2), I mixed some brilliant red artist's oil paint into the orange eggshell and painted it on top of the original orange base coat to give a darker and slightly warmer hue, leaving the masking tape in place and painting around it.

Mixing some oil-based scumble glaze with two-thirds burnt umber and one-third black artist's oil paint and white spirit, to the consistency of single cream, I brushed it over the table, starting with the top before doing the table edge and legs. I did a section at a time, adding shadows of burnt umber before removing the brush strokes with a pad of stockinette. Using an overgrainer, I pulled it

Orange eggshell paint mixed with brilliant red artist's oil paint, using a little white spirit to dilute the brilliant red oil paint.

The coffee table painted with the darker orange mix, leaving the square in the centre blank.

Oil-based scumble glaze mixed with two-thirds burnt umber and one-third black artist's oil paint with white spirit in a paint bucket.

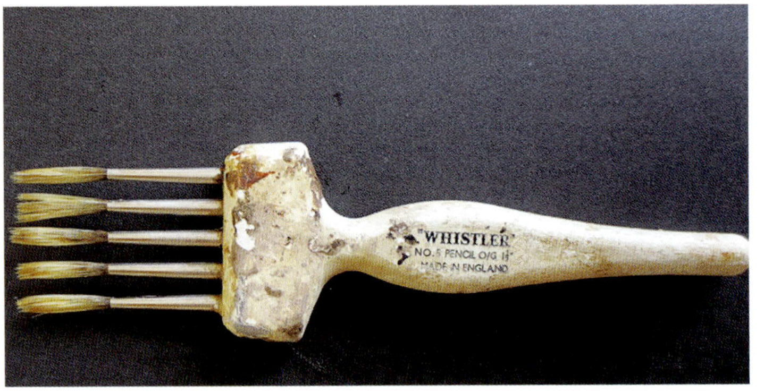

This brush is called an overgrainer and is a must-have brush for wood-graining.

Painted wood-graining softened with a badger brush.

The area darkened with burnt umber and wood-grained again using the overgrainer.

across the scumble using wobbly lines to give the impression of grain, before using my badger brush to soften the work. When softening your work with the badger brush, make sure to use the badger against the grain you have painted. You need to work quickly before the glaze becomes tacky.

Once this was dry, I added a thin coat of burnt umber diluted with a little white spirit over the top. I used a pad of stockinette to remove the brush marks before using the overgrainer again and badgering.

To paint a faux tortoiseshell effect to frame the central design on the tabletop, I painted a mix of yellow ochre and raw umber with a little white eggshell for the base coat. To make sure that the colour didn't seep, I put a strip of masking tape either side of the area I was painting.

The base coat colour painted onto the space left to frame the centre square on the table. A mix of yellow ochre, raw umber and a little white eggshell.

To paint the tortoiseshell effect, I mixed a light glaze with half raw sienna and half white spirit. Holding a small fitch very tightly, I made the marks by pulling the brush away from myself. Then I added in the burnt umber, keeping it fairly dry by only using a very small amount of white spirit. I painted it onto the area using a Cicat weave design, making sure that the strokes were all going in the same direction. I then took my badger brush and used it very gently, up and down, and then across the grain. I tore away the masking tape before the paint dried.

For the inside edge of the frame, I mixed burnt umber and black artist's oil paint with a tiny bit of scumble glaze and white spirit. I brushed it onto the area, making sure that the tortoiseshell effect was completely dry, and first sealing the edges with masking tape. I then used a pad of stockinette to remove brush marks and excess paint. I dragged a size 6, nylon-bristle fitch with no paint on from one edge to the opposite edge to make a faux grained effect. I then used a small, pointed artist's brush with burnt umber to paint an outline on the tortoiseshell frame.

The centre square remained white, waiting for the artwork. I chose a dried sprig of bay leaves as I liked the colouring with the wood effect as well as the sense of movement. After drawing the sprig on paper, I then traced it to position the design in the centre before painting the background for the artwork in the square. I used raw umber to complement the earth colours I had already used and mixed it with scumble glaze and white spirit to the consistency of single cream. I painted it carefully around the traced image, removing the brush marks with stockinette. Any drops that accidentally fall on the artwork can be wiped off with a little white spirit on a cloth or piece of kitchen roll.

The dried bay leaves were then hand-painted in artist's oil paints to complete the table (*see* Chapter 7).

Tortoiseshell effect painted on the outside edge of the frame.

A faux wood effect painted onto the inside edge of the frame using burnt umber and black artist's oil paint, a very small amount of white spirit and scumble glaze.

A mix of raw umber with scumble glaze and white spirit, painted on the central square, leaving the outline of the artwork clear, padded with stockinette to remove brush strokes.

PROJECT – CHEST OF DRAWERS

The preparation for this chest of drawers can be seen in Chapter 2. Once cleaned and sanded, I painted it with two coats of water-based chalk-white paint and then sealed it with a coat of water-based clear varnish. To achieve a good decorative paint effect, you need to be able to move the paint around smoothly and easily; the chalk paint would have absorbed the glaze and it would not have worked without varnishing.

Sample Board Experiments

Before painting the chest of drawers, I experimented on a sample board to check the type of effect I wanted. I painted three different types of paint effects, knowing that raw sienna was the pigment I would use as the main colouring for the chest of drawers.

I mixed some raw sienna pigment with a little water and then added water-based scumble glaze and stirred it together. It takes a little practice to get the correct consistency, but always aim for it to be the thickness of single cream. I brushed it onto the surface of the board and then, using a pad of stockinette, gently removed the brush strokes. I then twisted and rolled a small shammy leather so that the creases and curves would make an imprint in the glaze. Rolling the shammy from the top to the bottom makes an interesting pattern, resembling falling leaves.

Although I like the shammy leather effect, it works better on larger pieces, and I decided that it would be too big a design on the chest of drawers. For fun, I thought I would use the same mix of glaze again with a similar technique using bubble wrap to create a honeycomb design. After brushing the glaze onto the sample board and removing the brush marks with stockinette, I dabbed bubble wrap over the glaze.

I can imagine using this honeycomb effect on a child's table or chair, and adding bumble-bee decorations to give it added interest, but it wasn't what I wanted for the chest of drawers. It does show you, however, that experimenting with glaze is fun and if you don't like it you can wipe it off with a damp cloth. Try using a crumpled plastic bag, or with an oil-based glaze try using crumpled-up newspaper – there are endless possibilities.

Raw sienna pigment.

Tools and materials to be used for a distressed paint effect: water-based scumble glaze, a roll of stockinette, raw sienna pigment, a shammy leather, a paint bucket and a paint brush.

Raw sienna pigment and water-based scumble glaze with a little water, mixed together and painted onto a sample board.

Brush strokes removed using a pad of stockinette.

Twisting the shammy leather and rolling it over the glaze to make a distressed leafy effect.

The shammy leather rag-roll effect on the sample board.

For the third and final effect on my sample board in preparation for painting the chest of drawers, I first brushed on the same raw sienna with a little water and water-based scumble glaze. I then added streaks of raw umber and chalk white before padding all over with stockinette and then softening with a badger brush.

I then flicked droplets of water all over the badgered work and let it sit for a minute or two before badgering again. The droplets of water separate the glaze and you find you have an interesting stone effect. Although I decided that none of the three samples I had painted were exactly what I wanted on the chest of drawers, it led me to realise the effect that I did want. I didn't want a stone effect, but I did like the gentle combination of the raw sienna and raw umber blended gently together, but without the chalk white or the water droplets.

Using the same scumble mix as the shammy leather rag-roll sample and removing the brush strokes with a pad of stockinette, I imprinted bubble wrap on the glaze to make a honeycomb effect. If you try this, pad the bubble wrap straight up and down, being careful not to let it slip.

Water-based scumble glaze mixed with raw sienna pigment and a little water, brushed onto a sample board. Shadows using raw umber and chalk white were added with a brush before the brush strokes were removed using a pad of stockinette.

Creating the Chosen Paint Effect

Now I had decided on the colour and effect I was looking for, I mixed raw sienna pigment with a little water and scumble glaze in a paint bucket and, avoiding the outlines of the poppy seed heads I had loosely drawn on the top of the chest of drawers, I brushed the glaze on. With a separate brush, and while the glaze was still wet, I quickly brushed on shadows using raw umber. I used a damp, large fitch brush for the raw umber instead of making a mix of raw umber and water as I didn't want the glaze to get any wetter before I padded all over with stockinette. I then used the badger brush to soften it together, using it in different directions and moving it quickly, making sure that the bristles didn't go into the paint and leave brush marks.

When I decided to use poppy seed heads as the artwork, I put three poppy seed heads on the top to check for size, shape and so on (*see* Chapter 1). As I did so, lots of little poppy seeds rolled out and onto the surface of the chest of drawers. I realised that this gave it life, so I thought I would incorporate seeds into the painting. While the glaze was still wet, I dipped a small fitch brush into diluted black gouache and flicked the gouache onto the top, leaving it to sink

The distressed effect once the sample has been softened using the badger brush.

into the glaze. I flicked more gouache around the seed heads than the rest of the surface. When I start the artwork, I will add more, and the ones I let sink into the glaze will be pale in the background. Painting the poppy seed heads to complete the chest of drawers can be seen in Chapter 7.

Three distressed effects on the sample board, using raw sienna as the main colour.

Raw sienna pigment, water-based scumble glaze and water mixed together in paint bucket.

Brush strokes removed using a pad of stockinette, leaving the areas clear where the poppy seed head outlines were drawn.

Black gouache diluted with a little water flicked onto the glaze on the surface of the chest of drawers. Any spots that strayed onto the area left clear for the poppy seed head painting can be wiped off using a damp cloth.

Raw sienna glaze painted onto the surface of the chest of drawers, with raw umber shadows added.

The surface softened with a badger brush.

The top of chest of drawers with a distressed paint effect.

LAPIS LAZULI

Lapis lazuli is a beautiful blue rock, originating from northern Afghanistan as early as the seventh millennium BCE. By the Middle Ages and the Renaissance, lapis lazuli was ground down to make the pigment ultramarine, and Vermeer used it in his painting *The Girl with the Pearl Earring*. It was also often used in depictions of the Virgin Mary. Second to gold, it was the most expensive pigment available until the early nineteenth century when a chemically synthetic pigment became available. Highly polished, lapis lazuli is a perfect stone with which to make jewellery, boxes, ornaments and small statues. It seemed a good choice of stone to paint the four wooden knobs on the two-drawer chest.

Project – Two-Drawer Chest

I began by painting a small sample board with a light blue background base coat, using watercolour ultramarine and water-based white eggshell. At the same time, I painted a coat of the tinted blue eggshell onto the four wooden knobs.

Continuing with the sample board, I then painted on a mixture of ultramarine with white water-based scumble glaze and a little water, keeping the mixture quite thin. I made up a little yellow ochre and white on the palette and, dipping the tip of my goose feather into the mix, I painted on a faint vein, keeping it vague and not too distinct. Adding a little water to ultramarine, I next dipped a small sponge into the paint and sponged it onto the glaze, avoiding the veins I had just painted. A small

A sample board showing the base coat of water-based white eggshell tinted using ultramarine watercolour. The four wooden knobs are also painted with the same tinted base coat.

Ultramarine watercolour mixed with water-based scumble glaze and water, painted onto the sample board.

Veins added with the tip of a goose feather in yellow ochre and white mix.

A small sponge and slightly diluted ultramarine blue.

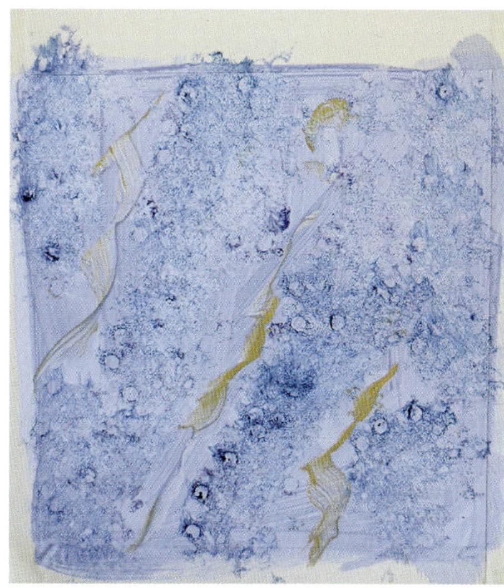

The ultramarine sponged onto the sample board, being careful not to sponge over the veins.

natural sponge is ideal; however, you could also cut pieces off a large decorating sponge as needed (as I did with this piece). You can't be impatient with lapis lazuli; it needs to be built up slowly while varying the weight and colour as you go.

Mixing some Prussian blue with a very small amount of water, I dipped the sponge in and sponged it over the ultramarine. Prussian blue is much darker and stronger than ultramarine. I then added some burnt umber to the Prussian blue and sponged it on. Once I had built up the ultramarine, Prussian blue and Prussian blue mixed with burnt umber, I dipped a small badger brush in water (just the tips of the brush) and spotted it over the sample board. I let it sit

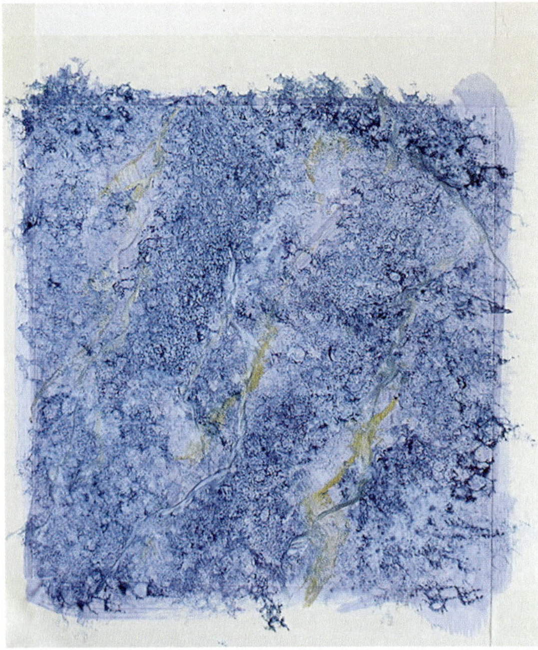

A sponge with Prussian blue was used to add to the body of the faux lapis lazuli.

Bronze powders in old bronze and gold were flicked onto the sample.

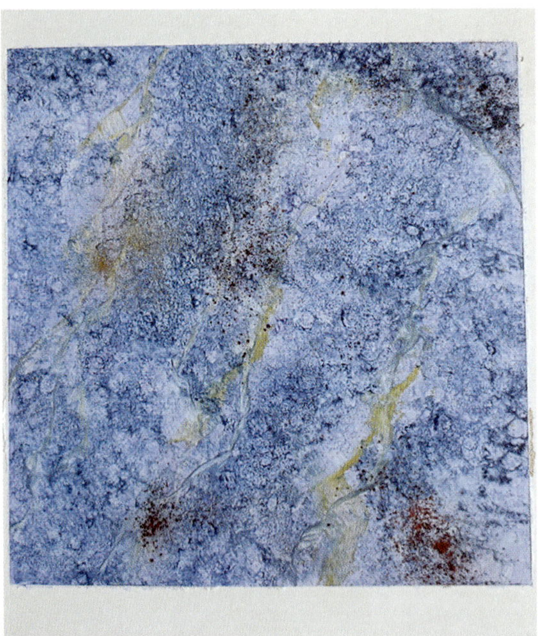

Lapis lazuli completed on the sample board.

Lapis lazuli is highly polished. To achieve this effect on the lapis-lazuli-painted knob, I used clear nail varnish.

for a few minutes and then dipped a small fitch (you could also use the tip of a goose feather) into the pale mix of yellow ochre and white, and added small veins before sponging again very gently. I finished the technique by dipping the end of the small badger brush into bronze powder; I used gold and old bronze, and flicked it carefully onto the faux lapis lazuli painting.

The finished knob to be attached to a two-drawer painted chest, alongside three further knobs painted in lapis lazuli.

CHAPTER 7

PAINTING ART DIRECTLY ONTO FURNITURE

Painting furniture is a timeless craft dating back centuries. The earliest examples have been found in tombs in Egypt, where furniture was painted with colourful, vibrant pigments and designs to show their wealth and status.

The art of furniture painting flourished in the Renaissance era and became a symbol of wealth with portraits, landscapes and fine art painted onto the wooden panels of furniture. Skilled craftsmen brought art into daily life by painting intricate and bold designs onto everyday pieces. Later, with the emergence of the Industrial Revolution, mass production altered the way that furniture was made, and so, the way it was painted. It nevertheless remained an important part of interior decoration and continued to add personalisation to each piece.

The Art Nouveau movement heralded another transformation in painted furniture with its geometric shapes, bold colours and abstract designs, with designs coming from American Indian, Egyptian and Early Classical sources from nature.

Painting art onto furniture is a wonderfully creative way to transform your furniture and breathe new life into it while stamping your own personality on it at the same time. Warm shades of paint – browns, greens and reds – inspired by nature are in vogue at the time of writing, which means this is a great time to paint your botanical artwork onto your favourite piece of furniture! The practicality of painting furniture has always been present, but even more so today with the craft we have now coined as 'upcycling'. Paint is transformational and can turn the drabbest piece into a work of wonder. Paint also, of course, covers wear and tear, and knots and gaps can be filled and sanded to reinvent an old piece to look like new.

Some of the furniture pieces I have painted are new, and some pieces are upcycled and reinvented with different colours and designs. This chest of drawers is from a commission painted a while ago, where the client asked for an Egyptian theme. It was an old chest of drawers, which suited this design and its lotus motifs, subtle paint colours and corresponding painted borders along the edges of the pull-out drawers.

A commission for an Egyptian-themed chest of drawers painted in subtle colours with Egyptian borders.

A peony loosely painted in artist's oil paints on the surface of an upcycled two-drawer chest.

CHILDREN'S

Project – Toy Box

When painting artwork directly onto furniture, several things need to be considered, as much depends on the surface you will be painting on and what technique you are using. It is very rare that I would use a water-based medium on furniture because it is not long-lasting. I prefer oil-based paints or enamel. I particularly like using enamels when stencilling. The general rule of thumb is that it is OK to paint oils on top of water-based paints, but it does not work the other way around.

The following toy box was ordered online for a client, and the finish on the box was spray-painted by the manufacturer in cream with the lid in wood. I was asked to add floral illustrations with the name of the child on the lid. The client wanted to make sure that it would not look out of place as the years went by; in other words, it should not be too childish.

Although I knew that the design should not be babyish, I also had to bear in mind that this had been ordered for a child, so I wanted to make it colourful and fun. I decided to use a limited palette of colours, mostly primary colours.

The panels on each end and the centre were slightly indented, leaving a perfect frame around each panel. I decided to frame the panels with large daisies positioned in different directions

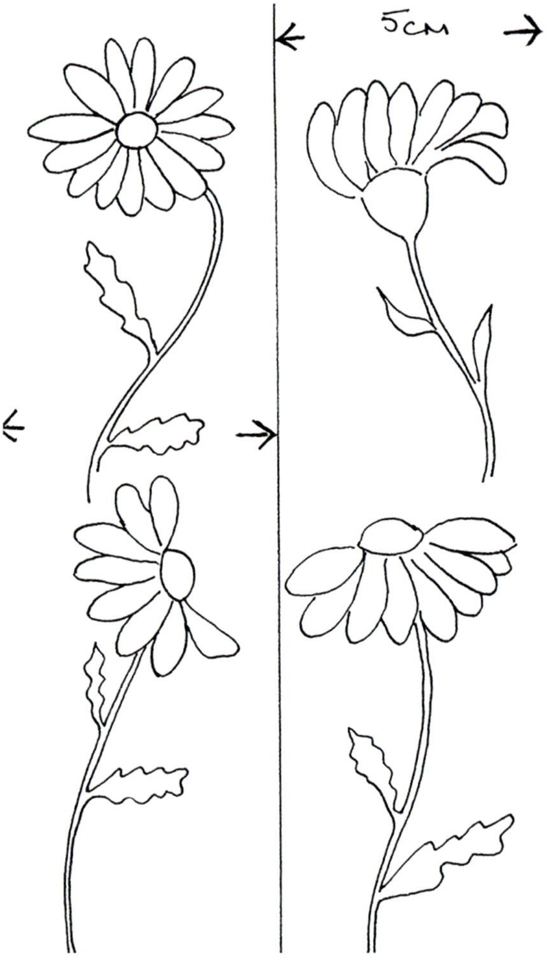

The outline of the design for the daisies before tracing, 5cm (2in) wide to fit on the side frames of the toy box.

The plain toy box before painting illustrations; note there is a 5cm (2in) frame around the edge.

to give the idea of movement. The width of the frame was 5cm (2in), so I drew the daisies I wanted to paint on a sheet of paper, making sure that they were the correct size.

The best way to put the outline of the daisies onto the toy box was to trace them (*see* Chapter 4). For the petals, I used white oil-based eggshell. It is hard-wearing and stays firm to the surface. It also provides a smooth base for any further colours to be painted on top. It is best to dilute some eggshell with a little white spirit and mix until it is the texture of single cream. I use washed-out plastic stock cups, which are a perfect size for mixing small amounts of paint.

I painted the leaves with a mixture of artist's oil paints, medium yellow and Prussian blue, with a little white spirit. I painted the green directly onto the cream base of the toy box using a small brush, plus a small, soft, dry brush to soften and move the paint around. Using a small soft brush to soften the green also helps to avoid leaving visible brush strokes. I painted the centre of the daisies with a medium yellow artist's oil paint directly onto the cream base.

When the white oil-based eggshell on the petals was dry, I painted a second coat. You need to leave the white eggshell to dry for at least twenty-four hours to make sure that the second coat goes on smoothly. This made the petals stand out and also hid any pencil marks that were still showing. Once the second coat was dry, I painted a little burnt umber around the base of the yellow pollen so it didn't look flat. When the burnt umber was dry (having

Daisy petals painted with a coat of oil-based white eggshell, mixed with a little white spirit to the consistency of single cream, making sure it wasn't runny enough to drip. The leaves are painted with a mix of medium yellow and Prussian blue, softened with a dry, soft brush.

Daisies with a second coat of white eggshell on the petals. I added burnt umber at the base of the central yellow disc and softened with a small, dry brush. I then added a little Prussian blue to the tops of the petals with a small brush, gently stroking the blue outwards.

been left for at least twenty-four hours to dry), I added a little Prussian blue oil paint to the tops of the petals. Using the dry, soft brush, I gently brushed it outwards towards the tips, moving the paint very carefully with the dry brush, building up the blue between the petals with a little less on the body of the petals. Adding a bit more colour gave the daisies more depth and presence. It also gave the impression of movement and lightness.

The panels at each end of the toy box needed to have a contrasting colour to the white daisies on the sides. As I had decided to keep the colours as primary as possible with a very uncomplicated palette, I thought a spray of red rowan mountain-ash berries would work well in the centre. A nice big clump filled up the space well, whereas if I had put a few single flowers there they would have looked lost and not had the same impact.

Measuring carefully to ensure the design was in the centre, I then used the same technique as with the daisies – tracing and then drawing the design onto the toy box.

As with the daisy petals, I painted the rowan berries with a coat of white oil-based eggshell mixed with a little white spirit. Don't make it so runny that it drips while you are painting. If you make a mistake, it is easy to wipe off with a little white spirit on a soft cloth. This makes the red stand out better and will also give a good impression of shine to the berries. The leaves and stalks were painted with the same mixture of medium yellow and Prussian blue as I used on the leaves for the daisies, and were softened with a small, dry brush, building the paint up to darken areas where necessary and along the veins. You can also dip a small pointed brush into white spirit (ensuring it is not too wet) and go over the veins, removing any green paint that shouldn't be there. I used the same image and process for the other end of the toy box, so that the ends are matching.

I now had to decide what to paint on the front of the toy box. I had already painted the daisies on the sides of the frame. I chose poppies as the central illustration. The red would be bright and cheery as well as carrying through

Berries painted with one coat of oil-based white eggshell mixed with a little white spirit.

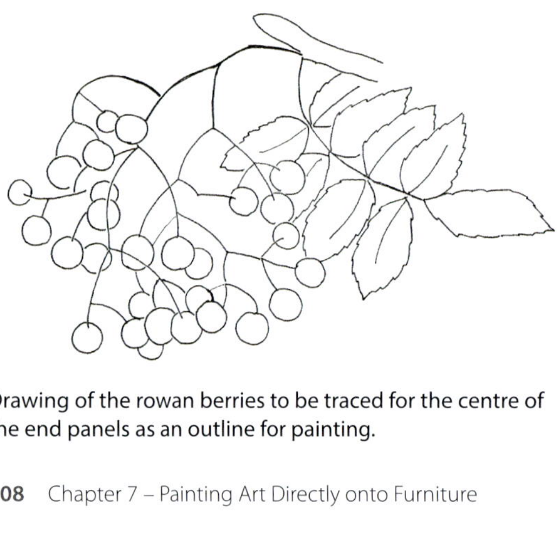

Drawing of the rowan berries to be traced for the centre of the end panels as an outline for painting.

The rowan berries framed with daisies on the end panel, with the stalk painted in burnt umber and raw umber.

the colour from the rowan berries painted on the ends of the toy box.

As with the daisies and berries, I drew the poppies, traced them, and transferred them onto the centre of the box, carefully measuring to make sure that they were centred. Again, as with the rowan berries and daisies, I painted a coat of oil-based white eggshell thinned with a little white spirit onto the petals. Once they were dry, I painted the petals with artist's brilliant red, using my soft, dry brush to move the paint around to build up dark and light areas, creating shine and depth with the white underneath.

Although the poppies stood out well on the front of the toy box, something else was needed to fill the space. I decided to paint a sprig from a juneberry shrub flowing downwards towards the poppies from the top-right and left-hand corners. The same process of tracing was used, and the petals were painted with two coats of oil-based white eggshell slightly thinned each time with white spirit. The leaves were painted with burnt sienna, which is a lovely earth colour, and darkened with a little burnt umber where necessary.

See Chapter 3 for the lettering for the name on the lid of the toy box.

Once the white eggshell was dry, I painted the petals in artist's oil paint brilliant red. I used a mixture of Prussian blue and brilliant red for the stigma in the centre.

A juneberry shrub painted in the top left-hand corner using oil-based white eggshell paint, burnt sienna and burnt umber artist's oil paints.

A sprig of juneberry painted on the top-right-hand corner on the front of the toy box, drawn onto the box by flipping the tracing from the left-hand side before painting. White oil-based eggshell paint, burnt sienna and burnt umber artist's oil paints.

The front of the toy box once the designs had been painted.

Project – Children's Rush-Seat Chairs

Painting botanical illustrations onto children's rush-seat chairs makes a good combination with the natural reed seats and wooden carcass. The chairs arrive unpainted and you can see how to paint them in Chapter 1. I usually paint a white background as it allows the artwork, names and dates of birth to stand out, as well as making sure that they blend with ease into any colour and design already present in the client's house. Where possible, I use a photograph of the flower/plant I am going to illustrate. The following acer chair is an example where the leaf designs were from a photograph I took, which helped with reference to shape and size. All the illustrations on the chairs were painted using artist's oil paints, and the names were painted with oil-based white eggshell mixed with a little artist's oil paint to achieve the correct colour.

Poppies are always a popular illustration to paint on children's rush-seat chairs, particularly if the child's name is Poppy! They make a bright and cheery design on furniture in any nursery.

Wildflower illustrations on rush-seat chairs are simple but effective, and are part of the wildflower range that is on my children's hand-painted furniture website, alongside the wildflower alphabet.

Delicate pink roses painted onto a rush-seat chair, personalised with the child's name on the front.

Acer leaves painted onto a rush-seat chair.

A photograph of acer leaves used as reference for painting the leaves onto the rush-seat chair.

Poppies painted onto a rush-seat chair personalised with the name of the child.

Wildflower design on a child's rush-seat chair personalised with the name of the child.

Project – Beatrix Potter-Themed Furniture

Beatrix Potter is a well-known writer, artist and botanist. Her first of many publications by Frederick Warne was the story of Peter Rabbit and his timeless adventures. Her illustrations are as popular today as they were at the outset, and the Beatrix Potter rush-seat chairs I paint are always in demand.

Using a light HP pencil, I drew the outline of Peter Rabbit onto the upright of the chair and began by painting a light wash of burnt sienna, mixed with a little white spirit. I then used a small soft brush to soften the paint. Next, with a little Prussian blue with white spirit, I painted a wash onto Peter Rabbit's jacket. I then used a small soft brush to move and soften the paint, creating areas of darker shadows.

Next, I painted a little burnt umber diluted with white spirit onto the top of Peter Rabbit's head. With a small soft brush, I moved and softened the burnt umber where darker areas give the rabbit more shape and depth. Then I used a small, pointed brush to paint the outline of Peter Rabbit with burnt umber artist's oil paint and to create more shadows on the fur under his jacket.

Materials for painting Peter Rabbit and other Beatrix Potter illustrations on children's rush-seat chairs. For Peter Rabbit, Prussian blue, burnt sienna and burnt umber artist's oil paints are used.

Painting a light wash of burnt sienna mixed with a little white spirit and then softening the paint.

Peter Rabbit's jacket in Prussian blue.

To finish the painting, I used alizarin crimson for the cotton reel, red for the kerchief and burnt sienna and burnt umber for the rabbits and mouse. The colour for the name is a mix of oil-based white eggshell and Prussian blue diluted with a little white spirit.

Adding burnt umber diluted with white spirit to the top of Peter Rabbit's head.

Softening the burnt umber to create depth.

Painting the outline of Peter Rabbit and creating further shadow.

The finished hand-painted Beatrix Potter chair.

Project – Tulip Wastepaper Basket

As described in Chapter 6, the dark faux mahogany background was painted using several layers. After layer one, I attached a template for the seed heads to leave the area pale for the artwork to follow.

Once the colouring for the faux mahogany background had been added, I began to paint the seed heads using white eggshell paint diluted with white spirit, neatening the tendrils and small areas behind the tendrils using raw umber and burnt umber artist's oil paint.

Once the white eggshell was dry, I worked a little more on the detail of the seed heads, using raw sienna artist's oil paint, burnt sienna and raw umber.

The cut-out template on white cartridge paper positioned on the bin to cover the area from the next layer of paint.

With the template attached to the bin using small pieces of masking tape, the next layer of red, raw umber and burnt umber was painted over the top and softened.

I removed the template, leaving a paler area for the seed heads to be painted.

The template after the red, raw umber and burnt umber had been painted over it.

Beginning to paint the seed heads with white eggshell, before adding detail bit by bit.

Adding more detail with yellow ochre and burnt sienna on the seed heads, with burnt umber in the spaces between the tendrils to neaten them up and help them stand out. I used a very fine brush to paint the detail on the coils of the seed head as well as the detail on the dried petals.

The finished piece, with more detail using Chinese white artist's oil paint to highlight areas where necessary on the seed heads.

Project – Bedside Cabinet

Once I had painted the frame around the top of the bedside cabinet in a faux porphyry stone, I traced my drawing of the blackberries I was going to paint to decorate the top. I had already painted the top with two coats of white oil-based eggshell as I intended to use artist's oil paint to paint the blackberries. The source of the design came from a photograph I took of a blackberry bush. I then drew the part of the bush I thought would work well as the design without it looking too cluttered.

I used a minimal palette of artist's oil-based paints, which included Prussian blue, alizarin crimson, burnt umber and brilliant red. I built up the colouring bit by bit, making sure that the light remained on the berries by leaving small white areas and softening the paint around it. I moved the paint into the darker areas as I softened the brush strokes. I slowly made the berries darker and richer by adding more paint and continuing to soften the paint as I worked.

The photograph I used as reference for the blackberry painting.

Having transferred the drawing using a tracing, I began to paint the blackberries, building up the colour using a palette of Prussian blue, alizarin crimson, burnt umber and brilliant red artist's oil paints.

Building on the detail and colours, adding a darker mix between each little segment/drupelet, keeping a small white area on each to keep a shine.

Adding detail using burnt sienna, raw sienna and burnt umber to the canes, coarse strands/ styles and the trichomes, while continuing to darken the fruit.

I painted the leaves using sap green with a little Prussian blue. The dark spots on the leaves were painted with burnt umber and burnt sienna, softened with a small brush.

Although the pencil outlines gave me a good guide, I also painted with the photograph of the blackberries on my computer screen for reference and to help with the detail where needed.

Once the art work was finished on the top of the bedside cabinet, I painted the remainder of the piece of furniture as faux porphyry (*see* Chapter 6).

Project – Chest of Drawers

Once the upcycled chest of drawers had been painted with chalk-white furniture paint and varnished (*see* Chapter 2), and the distressed decorative paint technique was dry (*see* Chapter 6), I was ready to paint the artwork.

I left loose spaces for the poppy seed heads when painting the decorative glaze, some smudged onto the space I had left, but this was easy to wipe off when wet with a damp cotton cloth.

An advantage of poppy seed heads is that they are light and easy to place on the surface of the chest of drawers to use as reference for painting. Putting each one beside the space I had left to paint each one, I did a quick sketch in pencil. I used a small palette of artist's oil paint in earth colours consisting of raw umber, burnt umber, burnt sienna and raw sienna. I collect lids from jars to use as palettes and put a little of each colour in one lid. I also use the same jar for white spirit all the time, topping it up when necessary. The paint drops to the bottom of the jar but the white spirit over time gets a little hazy and I prefer it that way.

I started the painting by using raw sienna as a base, and then mixing the raw sienna with burnt sienna to darken some areas. I then used burnt umber and raw umber to darken parts of the seed head in small areas where needed.

When I had painted the detail and felt that the paintings of the seed heads were complete, I painted poppy seeds around the seed heads. I didn't want to flick the paint, as I had when

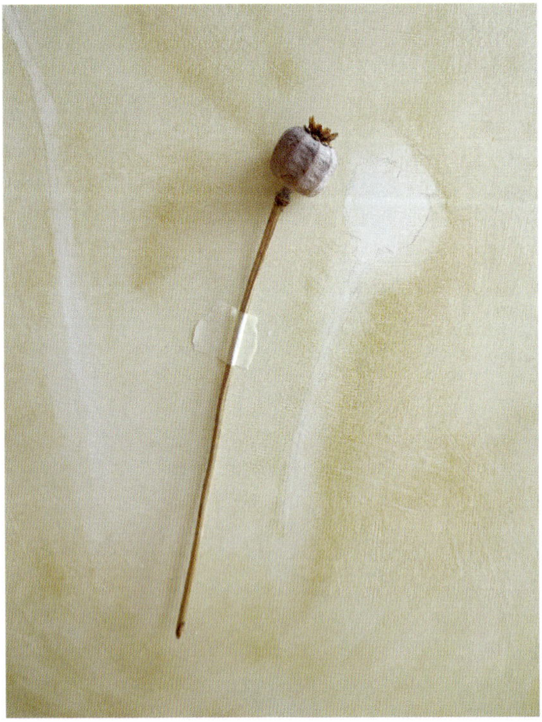

I attached the poppy with a small piece of masking tape to use as a reference next to the area I had left pale to paint the poppy seed head.

I had smudged a small area with the glaze over the outline of the seed head; here it has been wiped off with a damp soft cloth.

Adding some detail with a pencil to each of the three poppy seed heads before beginning to paint.

I began the painting with a pale layer of raw sienna and burnt sienna.

I then added burnt umber to the shadowed areas on the seed head.

I used a palette of burnt sienna, raw sienna, burnt umber and raw umber artist's oil paints to paint the poppy seed heads, with the lid of a jar and a jar of white spirit used for mixing the colours.

Dipping a calligraphy brush in black gouache, I dotted tiny black seeds around the tops of the seed heads, which stood out in front of the pale seeds I had dotted on before when the glaze was still wet.

The finished poppy seed heads with black painted seeds.

painting the decorative technique, as I wanted to avoid inadvertantly splattering the seed heads in the process. Instead, I used a thin calligraphy brush dipped in black gouache paint and, making sure the brush was upright, gently painted the seeds using the tip of the brush.

Once the poppy seed heads on the top of the chest of drawers were complete, I continued to paint poppy seed heads onto the sides of the chest of drawers. I then painted a line around the top using bronze metallic powder to finish (*see* Chapter 5).

The top of the chest of drawers showing the artwork and the rim painted around the top using bronze metal powder.

The finished chest of drawers, with the poppy seed heads on the top and on the sides.

Project – Two-Drawer Chest

This solid two-drawer chest was primed and painted in tinted eggshell paint, with holes filled on the front where old brass handles had once been, leaving one hole on each side for new knobs to be attached. *See* Chapter 6 for the lapis lazuli paint effect for the knobs and Chapter 5 for the detail around the base of the knobs.

A photograph of a wind-swept peony I used for reference.

Using a palette of alizarin crimson, Prussian blue, Indian red, medium yellow, raw sienna, yellow ochre, Chinese white and burnt umber I loosely painted the peony.

The tracing I used to transfer the outline of the peony onto the top of the chest for painting.

The two-drawer wooden chest before painting began.

The two-drawer wooden chest painted with tinted eggshell, peonies on the top and lapis-lazuli-painted knobs on the front.

For the artwork for the top of the chest, I chose a photograph from my photo library of a peony that was just on the turn. As you can see in Chapter 4, I enlarged the image on the monitor and traced both a blown-up version as well as a smaller version to transfer the images onto the chest.

Using a palette of Indian red, burnt sienna, raw sienna, alizarin crimson, Prussian blue and Chinese white artist's oil paints, I loosely painted the peonies onto the surface of the chest.

Project – Garden Coffee Table

Many years ago I worked and lived in Hong Kong for a short time and while there took some classes in Chinese painting. Once I had painted the faux Carrara marble in the centre of this coffee table, I painted groups of flower petals to decorate the green area on the tabletop, using a Chinese paintbrush and Chinese white artist's oil paint. When the white petals were dry the following day, I mixed some yellow ochre and raw umber into the white oil paint and painted some slightly tinted petals among the ones painted the day before.

The Chinese technique uses the size and weight of the brush to create depth and lightness. Putting the brush on the surface and pushing the bristles down creates the width; as you move it gently up until just the point of the brush is on the surface, you will have formed the shape of a leaf. Chinese brushes come in different sizes and the bristles are made from animal hair; most of the handles are made from bamboo but are also available in ceramic. It is worth looking after them carefully, and I always wash mine after use with warm water and washing-up liquid; even baby shampoo works well.

A garden table with faux Carrara marble and decorative floral artwork.

Detail of the petals showing the movement achieved using pressure up and down, and the tip of a Chinese paint brush. I used Chinese white, yellow ochre and raw umber artist's oil paints mixed with a little white spirit.

Ad Hoc Pieces

These fun tulips were painted in artist's oil paint on the panels of a door in a garden room in Chelsea. They stand out well with the frames being picked out with a green coloured oil-based scumble glaze.

There is much truth in the saying 'less is more' and this wastepaper basket is a good example. I painted the outer panels with black gloss oil-based paint and the inside with a cream eggshell. The top edge of the panels was rounded, which worked well with the design. The orange lines, giving the impression of a flower, were painted straight onto the panel of the basket with orange enamel paint. The contrast of the orange and black, along with the simplicity and flow of the lines, is eye-catching.

Simple lines painted in orange on a black gloss background.

Tulips painted onto the panels of a door in a garden room in Chelsea, with a corresponding green glaze brushed onto the bevelled frames on the door.

RESOURCES

Many of the materials used in this book, such as sandpaper, white spirit, paint buckets, etc., can be found in your local DiY store. However, I have compiled a list of suppliers, some of which are specialists in art and brush supplies, which I hope will help.

Acetate
londongraphics.co.uk

Badger brush
goldleafsupplies.co.uk
jacksonart.com

Bronze metals powders and gilt wax
goldleafsupplies.co.uk

Chalk paint
vintro.co.uk

Chinese artist paint brushes
justthebrush.co.uk

Enamel paint
https://uk.humbrol.com

Furniture paint
Most B&Q outlets
autentico-paint.co.uk

Gesso
jacksonart.com

Overgrainer
Available in 1, 2 or 3in sizes
flints.co.uk

Rabbit skin glue
jacksonart.com

Pigment
shop.stuartstevenson.co.uk

Water and oil based scumble glaze
www.brewers.co.uk

Shellac stain blocker
coo-var.co.uk

Spray mount
Amazon

Spray paint
Local B&Q

Stockinette
You may find it in your local garage or on Amazon

Transfer paper
Lazertran at Amazon

Whiting
jacksonart.com

INDEX

First published in 2025 by
The Crowood Press Ltd
Ramsbury, Marlborough
Wiltshire SN8 2HR

enquiries@crowood.com
www.crowood.com

British Library Cataloguing-in-Publication Data
A catalogue record for this book is available from the British Library.

ISBN 978 0 7198 44706

Cover design by Sergey Tsvetkov

Typeset by Envisage IT
Printed and bound in India by Thomson Press India Ltd.

Dedication

To Georgina and Edward who patiently grew up among the pigments and paint pots.

For further information about the author, visit:

www.sarahsherringtondesign.com (botanical art)
www.sarahsherrington.com (children's hand-painted furniture)